Secret Agents

SECRET AGENTS

How the top real estate agents list more, sell more & DOMINATE THE MARKET!

Lisa B.

Disclaimer

First Edition 2017

Copyright © 2017 by Lisa B

The moral rights of the author have been asserted

All inquiries should be made to the author.

National Library of Australia Cataloguing-in-Publication entry

Creator: B., Lisa, author.

Title: Secret agents: how the top real estate agents list more, sell more, & dominate the market! / Lisa B.

ISBN: 9781925471069 (paperback)

Subjects: Real estate agents.

Internet marketing.

Branding (Marketing)

Real property—Marketing.

Dewey Number: 333.33

Published with support by Author Express

Testimonials

"It's about actively capturing leads and going where they are, so you can connect with them. If you don't get smart about this, because this is exactly what Lisa does, she gets you smart about it. This is no longer an option it's a necessity. The clock is ticking, but there's still time to get smart and by smart I mean learning from someone like Lisa, because she has figured it out so you don't have to."

Mal Emery
The Millionaire Maker and Bestselling Marketing Author

"Lisa knows her stuff, it's that simple. With every man, woman and their respective canines touting themselves as 'social media experts' it's refreshing to find someone who walks her talk, and actually does what she teaches. Thanks for the help Lisa, much appreciated."

Glenn Twiddle
Glenn Twiddle - Sales Training

"Lisa has a wide range of digital marketing skills, and as a real estate agent herself they are incredibly practical to implement, and they work! She is an engaging writer (she writes a column for my magazine) and a gifted trainer, making the complex seem incredibly easy. If you're in Real Estate and want to learn how to attract more customers to your website and generate quality leads online, you only need to do one thing - call Lisa!"

Samantha Mclean
Editor - Elite Agent Magazine

Dedication

To Max

My little boy. My inspiration. My motivation.
My love.

My little best friend.

To My Mr Big

My rock. My smile.
My big best friend.

Acknowledgements

Thank you to the profession I love called real estate. Real estate has been extremely good to me over the years. I've had such a wonderful career with many exciting challenges and rewards. I've also met some great people who have become lifelong friends.

I wish to acknowledge the following people who have helped me throughout my lengthy real estate career.

To Alex Edler – Thank you for giving me my first real job in real estate. Thank you for the opportunity – the rest is history.

Thank you to all my employees over the years. I had some truly great people work with me and I learnt a lot from you all. In no particular order of appearance - Danyelle, Megan, Lynne, Bruce, Ben, Paul, Olga, Jim, Melissa, Lyn, David, Neil, Peter, Rodney, Emil, Liz, Katie, Alex, Bridie, Claire, Nevanka, James, Ivo, Margaret, Sharon, Lucas, John, Rod, Pam, Darryl, Ameilia, Lachlan plus many others. Thank you.

To the many vendors and purchasers who allowed me to help them with selling and buying their home. I felt very privileged and blessed every day.

Thank you to the many real estate agents I have been able to help with their marketing ideas and strategies. Thank you for seeing outside the box. I'm proud of you all for stepping up.

Thank you to my little family and my amazing friends for supporting me with their love and friendship.

Lisa

A SPECIAL GIFT FOR YOU!

Lisa would like to thank you and support you further by offering you Secret Agents in audio format.

That means you can listen to Secret Agents in the car, on your phone or computer.

Please go to www.TheRealEstateHotline.com.au/audiobook to collect your free audio book.

Contents

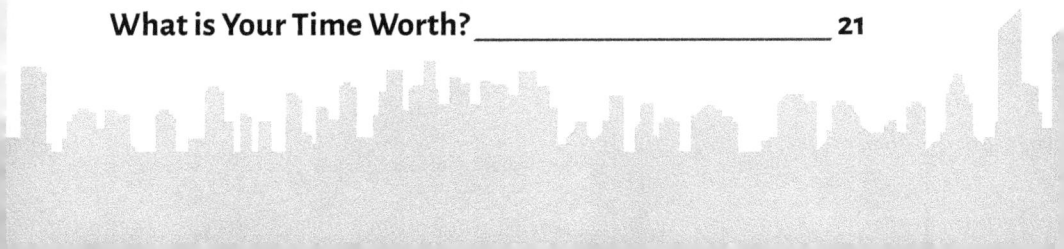

CONTENTS

CONTENTS

Secret Agents never rely on ONE way to make their phone ring.

Secret Agents make sure that marketing causes their phone to ring from MANY different sources.

Introduction

Welcome to *Secret Agents*

There are two types of secret agents.

The first is the agent that no one knows. They are invisible to their marketplace and no one has ever heard of them.

The second is the one that you want to be – they are the ultimate trained professional. They go about their business of taking over their market with almost military precision. They have systems and strategies. To the outside world no one quite knows what they're doing, but it's obvious they seriously dominate their market.

We're about to find out what they do.

This book has been specifically compiled to assist real estate agents to market both themselves and their business in order to attract customers. This information takes into account both offline and online marketing methods.

I will demonstrate how to optimise real estate websites in order to be found on predominant localised pages within the search engines. Remember, just because you build a website, it doesn't mean people will find it.

In the following pages, I will discuss how to massively improve the overall marketing of your real estate business online. This plan takes into account your ability to achieve the desired results.

My overall concept with online marketing has been defined as addressing the needs, in particular, of real estate businesses and their websites.

These ideas have been formed as the result of consultation with others and through research conducted during my long experience, together with extensive training in both online marketing and real estate practices, and my knowledge of real estate businesses, industry dynamics, competition, current and future technology and the history of the marketplace.

Before we begin, I must stress that all marketing strategies need to be monitored, results need to be measured and improvements identified and implemented. Furthermore, achieving results online can take time, and if rushed or achieved by way of disreputable practices it can lead to your pages being penalised or thrown off the internet.

Please note that the information we discuss about the online world is not meant to replace your offline marketing efforts. You must ensure that you have a mixture of both sources.

In this book I have included an important section that covers why we need to have several ways to make the phone ring; as Warren Buffet says, "Never depend on a single income. Make investment to create a second source."

My logic is you can't rely on one way to make the phone ring. If that one way ceases to work for whatever reason, you will have no leads and no enquiries.

We will now explore the overall concept of marketing for real estate agents and how to ensure that we have 'multiple streams of enquiry'.

For further information please visit –
www.TheRealEstateHotline.com.au

<2>

THE REAL ESTATE HOTLINE

Where salespeople and office principals call for advice and help regarding real estate sales, listings and marketing.

- 🔒 Have you run out of ideas on how to get a listing across the line?
- 🔒 Have you run out of ideas on how to get a sale across the line?
- 🔒 Do you need some marketing tips?
- 🔒 Are you having staff problems?
- 🔒 Are you new in sales?
- 🔒 Feeling overwhelmed?

Don't worry you can call us.

We have your back

The Real Estate Hotline
www.TheRealEstateHotline.com.au

On demand real estate coaching

Secret Agents build their online profile;

they know that everything they add online becomes a LISTING TOOL.

They demonstrate and PROVE their experience online to help win more business.

Part One:
Lead Generation

What are Multiple Streams of Enquiry?

This is the reward that you will receive as the result of adopting successful marketing strategies.

As real estate agents, we are employed to market our owner's property to attract buyers AND we are employed to negotiate the best possible price for the seller.

We are now going to discuss the first part of our role in great detail.

Marketing for real estate agents

In a real estate office, focus needs to be on marketing our properties for sale, marketing our offices and, of course, marketing ourselves. When we are focused on having multiple streams of enquiry, this allows us to have confidence in attracting future business. And for some of us, it means being able to break away from the feeling of reliance we place on the real estate portals.

The purpose of marketing is to make the phone ring for multiple reasons. It is helping the consumer get to know you and helping them choose you above your competition. Therefore you must also be marketing yourself! You are your brand, so you need to stop hiding and make sure that your marketplace knows who you are.

The intention of marketing is to make YOU memorable.

By the way, if you haven't read the book *Purple Cow* by Seth Godin, **buy it now.**

<5>

Marketing should constantly increase the value of your business. Whether you have invested your time, money or both, you must be able to quantify a return on your investment. You must be able to envisage future income by projecting how much your marketing will be monetised via qualified leads. You also need to incorporate a path for building future capital in your business.

Marketing must **cause** your phone to ring in numerous ways. You simply MUST have **multiple streams of enquiry.** If you don't, you are putting yourself in the very dangerous and vulnerable position of relying on third-party businesses for your leads.

In the past, many agents relied on newspapers in the same way that many now rely on real estate portals. If you don't have a marketing plan and a plan to generate multiple streams of income, you could find yourself held to ransom. You may find yourself having to succumb to the demands of the various portals. Their demands could be financial (increased fees) or they could require more information (property data).

The other danger, of course, is that they could change their business model at any time and start charging you for things they previously didn't. For example, they could start charging you for leads generated through their site. Worse still, they could open their own franchised offices or totally change the real estate business model. Remember, taxi drivers thought they were safe too before Uber came along.

What's the solution?

What you are reading is a detailed marketing plan that will give you ideas on how you can make your phone ring in a number of ways and for a variety of reasons. This will ensure that you build on your investment, giving you a solid guarantee and peace of mind for future income.

<6>

Your marketing plan is to be achieved encompassing both online and offline methods.

Remember that in order to have a long and successful career in real estate, you need to have a constant source of listings.

How to Use This Book

When you see a box like this □ tick off the suggestions that you have already in place and the things that you implement as you go.

How to Create Multiple Streams of Income in your Real Estate Business

12 ways to ensure future income in your business

- □ **1.** General Marketing
- □ **2.** Referral Programs
- □ **3.** Listings Sources
- □ **4.** Follow-up and Action Plans
- □ **5.** Anniversary Programs
- □ **6.** Welcome to the Neighbourhood Letter
- □ **7.** Absentee Owners
- □ **8.** Sales Team and New Business Managers
- □ **9.** Property Management
- □ **10.** Database – An Asset
- □ **11.** Training
- □ **12.** Additional Divisions to Complement your Office

<7>

1. General marketing

Always test your results for the return on your investment.

How are you getting your name out into the marketplace? How are you creating top-of-mind awareness so that the consumer remembers you? Listed below are various ways to create brand awareness in your marketplace.

- ☐ **For sale signs.** Have as many signs up on busy roads as you can – especially Sold signs.
- ☐ **Office window display.** Create innovative posters and displays – get creative! For example, at Christmas start a tradition to have your window display as a nativity scene or similar. Have it so amazing that people bring their children to look.
- ☐ **Keyrings**. Have company keyrings made – give them out to buyers, sellers and at every appraisal.
- ☐ **Internet**. Constantly market yourself online – this will be explained further as we continue.
- ☐ **Signs on cars.** Company cars with your office signage.
- ☐ **Brochures/newsletters/cards**. Marketing material constantly dropped in your area.
- ☐ **Brand**. Keep your brand and logo consistent EVERYWHERE.
- ☐ **Your company website**. Make it amazing. It's your company resume.
- ☐ **Your own personal website.** Make it amazing. It's your personal resume.
- ☐ **Advertising in newspapers.** Monitor the results for ROI.

<8>

- ☐ **Advertising in real estate portals.** Monitor the results for ROI (monitor premium listings, and so on).

- ☐ **Pre-pamp/introduction letter to appraisals.** Deliver with chocolates/gifts and make your first impression memorable.

- ☐ **Promotions with free giveaways.** Organise client nights, BBQs, Easter egg hunts, etc.

- ☐ **Giveaways.** Mugs/hats/T-shirts/umbrellas.

- ☐ **Gifts.** On exchange of contracts, take a photo of the buyer and seller standing in front of the property with their Sold sign. Shortly after exchange of contracts, give a photo in a nice frame to the seller and the buyer.

- ☐ **On exchange of contracts.** Give both the buyers and sellers a gift to celebrate; for example, a nice bottle of wine with your label (buy cleanskin wine and have your own label printed).

- ☐ **Offers**. Offer free statistical information or price comparisons to anyone thinking of buying or selling, as well as your free localised report (more on that later).

- ☐ **Give a gift at settlement** to the buyers and sellers... Wow them!

- ☐ **Follow-up.** Have your sales assistant follow up your buyers and sellers AFTER exchange of contracts and settlement, once the property is unconditional. This is the time to really show you are different to other agents. It will also stop any potential problems happening with settlement, as the buyers

<9>

and sellers will be informed. Going above and beyond at this point is where the REAL sales will be made with future referral business.

☐ **Local journalists.** Supply your local property journalists with real estate news. Let them know what's happening in your area - they may decide to include your information in their news articles.

☐ **Trade shows.** Participate in trade shows.

☐ **Information nights**. Run information nights for buyers and sellers. You could also run a virtual summit.

☐ **Network.** Make sure you always have business cards on hand to give out **when appropriate.**

☐ **Thank you cards.** Send thank you cards to everyone you speak to – buyers, sellers, landlords and so on.

☐ **Thank you letters.** After you list a property, make sure you send out a nice letter thanking them for their business.

☐ **Maintain contact**. Keep in touch with past and potential clients.

☐ **Promote local businesses on your website.** Offer this as a free service.

☐ **Phone numbers online.** Promote your company in the online phone book. Don't spend a lot on this – just use the basic advertisement.

☐ **Mini-mag.** Have your own real estate mini-magazine.

<10>

- ☐ **Bus and Billboard advertising.** Promote your business on local buses or billboards (sometimes you can obtain this very cheaply for a year's contract).

- ☐ **Free gifts**. Mugs; keyrings; hats; pens; statistics; price comparisons; chocolates; photo frames; welcome baskets; bottles of wine (with your label); books; T-shirts; newsletters; shopping bags; lollies; mints; offer to promote local businesses on your website.

Secret Agents always ask for referrals.

Secret Agents develop referral programs and they ALWAYS ask for referrals.

2. Referral programs

How do you obtain referrals for new business?

You should always ask for referrals. **Always.**

- ☐ Build relationships with local businesses. Ask them to refer sellers.

- ☐ Ask for referrals on your website.

- ☐ Ask for referrals on your social media sites (where appropriate).

<11>

☐ If allowed in your area, you could offer your administration and sales staff incentives for referring business to the office – for sales and property management leads.

☐ Offer referrals to local agents (if allowable in your area). If they are about to lose a listing, suggest they refer their seller to you and pay them a referral fee.

☐ Build relationships with industry experts: removalists, banks, solicitors, finance/ accountants, trades, etc. Refer each other's business (more on this later).

☐ Offer incentives for agents in your franchise or other real estate networks. You could offer a slightly higher referral fee, or offer to pay their referral fees on an unconditional contract.

☐ With every email and letter that goes out of the office, ask for referrals by including a short paragraph at the bottom of all of your correspondence.

☐ Ask for referrals from every seller and buyer you speak to.

☐ Ask for referrals on the back of your business card. You could put something like, 'If anyone you know is considering selling a property, please think of me.'

☐ Also, remember to always refer 'out of area' sellers to an agent who is located near the property for a referral fee (if appropriate in your area). Keep a register to monitor your referrals to other agents.

<12>

3. Listing sources

If you want to make money, chase listings. List them, then sell them. It all comes down to chasing and securing the listing.

When you have great houses for sale (that are reasonably priced), it's an easy way to make the phone ring.

So, in order to achieve this, you have to prospect for listings. How much time you need to spend doing this will depend on how well you have set yourself up in the past and whether you have been working on generating referrals and repeat business.

If you don't have the luxury of having a constant source of sellers contacting you to list their property for sale, you must canvass for new business. How much time you spend (the percentage of time) will depend on what position you are in.

If you drastically need stock, you might need to canvass for new business for 70 per cent of your allocated work time and then spend the remaining 30 per cent dealing with buyers. If you have a lot of stock and you need to focus on selling it, you might spend 60 per cent of your time with buyers and 40 per cent looking for new business. You need to have a balance that will work for where you are positioned with stock and sales at the time.

Here are some listing sources you can actively follow:

- ☐ **For sale by owner.** Approach private sellers and see if you can help them.

- ☐ **For rent by owner.** Approach landlords advertising online or in the paper to see if they would consider selling.

- ☐ **Expired listings.** Properties that were for sale and have now been taken off the market.

- ☐ **Past appraisal follow-up/action plan.** Keep in contact with all past appraisals.

- ☐ **Appraisals from former staff members**. There may be appraisals that were conducted in your office by agents who don't work there any more. Make sure that someone is keeping in contact with all past leads.

- ☐ **Ask around.** Ask every single buyer and seller you speak to if they know of anyone who has a property to sell.

- ☐ **Developers.** Keep in contact with developers. Keep a lookout for council development applications – this will give you a great insight into knowing what's happening in the area.

- ☐ **Generic office advertisements**. Come up with creative ways to make the phone ring.

- ☐ **Letterbox drops.**

- ☐ **New listings or sales**. When you have a new listing or sell a property, canvass around the property for sellers.

- ☐ **Areas of high turnover.** Generally, areas with a high turnover of properties are busy streets or very steep blocks – canvass them.

- ☐ **Phone prospect your enquiry log.** Obtain permission to keep in contact with buyers and sellers to help them find a property. Ensure that you are keeping in contact with your warm leads; have a system in your office where you make sure all buyers are followed up until they buy.

<14>

☐ **Please note:** Also remember to ask every enquiry that comes into the office for permission to include them in your email alerts.

4. Follow-up / action plans

Don't forget your warm leads; there are a number of reasons to keep in contact with people whom you have dealt with in the past. These people can be grouped together in an automated follow-up system.

☐ Appraisals

☐ Listings you have for sale

☐ Listings that have been withdrawn from sale

☐ Sales that are moving forward to settlement

☐ Established clients

☐ Local businesses

☐ Birthdays of past clients (this information can be collected with their permission on your sales advice letter)

Aim to have systems in place whereby your office will automatically follow up groups with specific targeted action plans. Each individual group will receive a series of letters, emails, phone calls, gifts, and so on.

Create **standout** follow-up procedures. Follow-up procedures will ensure that people remember you. This will also ensure you have a steady stream of listing enquiries.

<15>

5. Anniversary program

Become the agent that sellers remember. Organise a follow-up plan whereby people who have purchased property in your area receive an anniversary card.

- ☐ Send anniversary cards to people who have previously bought through your office. Send the card to arrive on the anniversary date they settled on the property.

- ☐ Add into your database, street by street, all the people who have bought in your area and the anniversary of the date they purchased (if you can source the details as to when they bought their home). Each year send them a card to say, for example, 'Congratulations, it's now been 7 years since you purchased your home.' It's highly unlikely that the agent they purchased through will do this. There is a great chance that the sellers will remember you as the agent who sold them the property.

- ☐ In your office, always have marketing projects running in the background. If your PA or secretary is quiet with their workload, they can continue with projects relating to your marketing. You can also outsource your marketing.

Secret Agents automate their follow-up systems.

They make it easy to keep in contact with past and future clients.

<16>

6. Welcome to the neighbourhood - Welcome pack

When people move into your area, whether you sold them the property or not, give them a welcome pack.

Your welcome pack could include:

- ☐ Discount vouchers from local businesses.
- ☐ Information about local schools.
- ☐ Information about doctors and other professionals.
- ☐ Let them know when rubbish/bin night is, and so on.
- ☐ Any other essential local information – get creative!
- ☐ You could also offer to include them in your Facebook community page (more on that later).

Prepare your welcome pack:

- ☐ Design a letter that welcomes them to the area.
- ☐ Organise your welcome pack and fill it with local area knowledge, gifts, etc.
- ☐ Include them in your anniversary action plan.

Again, chances are that the agent they purchased the property through will not do this.

7. Absentee owners campaign

Send information about what's happening in your area to absentee owners; that is, property owners who live in another area.

In doing this, when the sellers are ready to sell, they will remember you. As an example, I have had a number of investment properties located in different areas to where I live. I have NEVER heard from any of the real estate agents operating out of those areas. They have never told me about how the market was in their area.

<17>

What if one of the properties I owned was worth a lot more than I thought? I might decide to sell AND they could make a sale.

As an absentee owner, when I was ready to sell who would I list with? Someone who has taken an interest in my property. Someone who has sent me market updates; someone who has kept me informed; someone who has thought about ME.

Now to prepare:

- ☐ Prepare your 'Market Update Newsletter'. Include all the recent sales in the area, both yours and all of the other agents. Don't specify who sold each property - keep it generalised and print the information on your letterhead.

- ☐ Separate your farm area into pockets. Choose three areas to target. Send absentee owners a market update every three months.

8. Sales team and new business managers

Build a strong sales team. Always be on the lookout for good staff. Promote in various ways.

- ☐ Advertise positions vacant on your company website.

- ☐ Advertise for staff in your office windows/posters.

- ☐ Always be on the lookout for good people, such as at appraisals, for example.

- ☐ Advertise positions vacant in the paper, at job agencies, and so on.

- ☐ Advertise positions vacant on all of your social media channels.

<18>

9. Property management

Use similar strategies to increase your property management department. Build your asset base. Build a strong tangible, saleable asset.

10. Database asset

Build your online business. You MUST keep a record in one central location of every single buyer and seller who contacts your office. This is guaranteed when you have an enquiry log located at reception and you ensure that your office only promotes ONE phone number on your advertising and sign boards. Have your receptionist ask every single buyer enquiry for permission to add their details to your email alerts.

Always work on building your database, improving your website and increasing your overall online presence. This will be worth money to you. Your aim is to build an automated way to get listings. Also, when you want to sell your real estate business, it will be an attractive asset to any potential purchaser.

11. Training

Always attend training, and if you are a principal organise training for your staff. Topics to note:

- ☐ Prospecting – new lead generation
- ☐ Presenting – listing
- ☐ Marketing
- ☐ Follow-up
- ☐ Sales, closing and qualifying leads
- ☐ Time management

<19>

☐ Mindset

☐ Training, knowledge and growth

Increasing your skills will be an investment in future sales. Aim for a small increase of 10 per cent in each area. This will be worth thousands!

12. Franchising, marketing groups, finance, property management, strata management

Here you have a few questions to answer:

🔒 Will you open another office?

🔒 Do you have aspirations to create a franchise or marketing group?

🔒 Will you add a finance division to your office?

🔒 Will you add a strata management division to your office?

Develop your own Prospecting Plan

Create your own prospecting plan to work every day.

An example to start with:

☐ Send your buyer/alert newsletter out every week.

☐ Make sure you add names to your database daily.

☐ Ensure your online profile (your website and your information online) is amazing.

☐ Employ someone to deliver 1000 brochures a day, five days a week = 5000 a week.

<20>

☐ Have your admin/personal assistant make contact with absentee owners. Send reports and updates on the market.

☐ Canvass 'withdrawn from sale' properties – religiously.

☐ Add every single buyer who calls your office into your enquiry log. Make sure the buyers are followed up until they buy. **Always** ask if they are selling a property. (And again, make sure you have permission to contact them.)

☐ Devise your own plan that works for you. There are many ways to prospect for new business. As you progress online and your marketing momentum builds, you will have more and more things you can add to your online marketing strategies.

What is Your Time Worth?

When you are organising your marketing plan and you have organised the tasks YOU are committed to doing, it is essential to consider what YOUR time is worth.

Wasting our time is not only wasting our money; it's wasting our life.

Before you start to fold letters, drop brochures into letterboxes or do any kind of administrative task, you must assess what YOUR time is worth. In real estate, we quite often spend countless hours with 'potential clients'. We show them properties and sometimes they don't buy what we show them. We sometimes appraise the same property five times and the owners never sell. Sometimes potential vendors do not bring us a return on our time invested.

We can start to undervalue our time; this is when we need to get clear on what our time is really worth.

<21>

We need to look at our time this way: If we want to bring in, say, $300,000 for the year, let's work out the value we should place on our time.

The way we need to do this is to work out how many hours a week we would like to work.

Let's say, for the purpose of the exercise, we only wanted to work 30 hours a week. We will then work out what our hourly rate will be to earn that kind of money.

$300,000 divided by 52 weeks is $5770 per week.
$5770 divided by 30 hours is $192 per hour.

If our time is worth $192 an hour, consider what tasks we should and shouldn't be doing in those 30 hours. This will help us to see the value of engaging a personal assistant or a virtual assistant to help us with tasks where we know that we could employ someone for less than our valued rate; someone who will take the burden off us and allow us to concentrate on excelling at our chosen skills.

In this example, we would need to value our time at $192 per hour. So before we engage in the physical task of, say, dropping brochures in letterboxes, it makes sense to analyse what our time is worth.

Instead of delivering your own brochures, I suggest that you pay a company that specialises in brochure delivery; that way you will pay someone much less than your hourly rate. This leaves you to concentrate your efforts on income-producing tasks, such as listing appointments with qualified leads and buyer appointments with qualified buyers.

Don't waste time doing anything that you can pay someone else a lesser rate to do.

<22>

☐ Calculate how much your time is worth, based on the above example.

Secret Agents know that time is money – They spend both wisely.

<23>

Personal branding is critical.

Invest in your own personal website. Your personal website is about YOU. It's your online resume that you will add to forever.

Part Two:
Online Marketing

Before we examine the area of online marketing, we need to consider some important points.

Our priority, though not our sole agenda, is to gain a higher prominent ranking for your website in the natural search engine results, using Google as the main search engine. Our optimisation techniques will also enhance your ranking with the other leading search engines.

We have chosen Google simply because a higher percentage of Australians use Google as their preferred search engine. So for the purposes of this book, Google is King.

Why be Online?

You need to know WHY you must actively promote your business online. You must also keep in mind that without a strategy there really is no point in doing so.

13 major reasons why you must market yourself online

1. To work ON your business, as opposed to working IN your business.

2. To attract online customers; to attract online leads and online sales.

<25>

3. To add fresh content and include up-to-date information for Google.

4. Create opportunities. It's not who you know online, it's who knows you.

5. Build brand awareness. Every day you are building on your brand.

6. SEO strategies; staying on page one of Google – dominate the internet.

7. It's where your customers are hanging out.

8. Build relationships.

9. Position yourself as the expert.

10. Get known. Get to know people in the right places.

11. Develop a massive online history for YOU and YOUR company. This is your online resume.

12. Be the first in your area in real estate and stand out from the crowd. The one who claims the online space first will own it in the area and they will be remembered.

13. Brand protection.

What do you want from your online presence? What will you achieve?

- **Leads** – without having to prospect.
- **Listings** – converted more easily.
- **Sales** – with fewer problems.
- **Repeat business** – a following of raving fans.

<26>

Objectives of Your Marketing Plan

The purpose of marketing is to demonstrate to potential clients your value proposition in order to entice them to consider buying your services or products.

In the online world it is no different. You want to use all of your available programs and resources to drive leads back to your site.

The objective is to '**Dominate the Internet'** in your market. You must expose your business online and build a massive online profile the RIGHT way.

We all know you can't sell a secret. So, therefore, it stands to reason that YOU can't be a secret either. You can't hide behind your logo any longer.

You MUST become **famous** in your marketplace. That is the key. When people know you, like you and trust you, you will secure more business than you ever thought possible.

Search Engine Optimisation

We want to see your website at the front of search engine results with the leading search engines for selected keyword phrases. Our aim is to have you **organically listed in Google.**

This means that you don't have to pay for the privilege of being on page one. You EARN the right to be there.

To make this happen, particular pages of your website will need to be **optimised**. This will then attract quality sales leads that will result in more enquiries and, therefore, more listings and more sales.

<27>

☐ Again, please remember this: **always** drive traffic to YOUR website. Never direct any traffic to real estate industry portals. They don't need your help.

All of your marketing should aim to direct traffic to your main hub, your website. This is where you want to capture leads. This is where you want to make sales. This is your business. Your website IS your business.

In delivering higher levels of qualified traffic, not only will more buyers and sellers see your website but more people will see the properties you have for sale. It also makes sense that if you have your website at its optimum in terms of functionality, you will also make more sales and attract more listings.

Remember to claim your free audio version of secret agents

www.TheRealEstateHotline.com.au/audiobook

<28>

Where to Start with the Online World

Protect and prepare

Build your foundations. Just like a house has foundations, you also need to build a solid foundation for your online profile. You need to make sure that you build on everything you create.

Go to these two websites and follow the instructions to create the following two alerts:

- ☐ Google Alerts Register - www.google.com/alerts
- ☐ Twilert Register - www.twilert.com

On both registers, set individual alerts for the following keywords:

- ☐ Your name
- ☐ All of your staff; their individual names
- ☐ Your company name
- ☐ Suburbs in your trade area
- ☐ Your region

These alerts will let you know when anyone uses those words on the internet. By registering with these two programs and selecting some relevant keywords, you will be generating a report that will be sent to you on a daily basis. Elect to have it sent to you once a day.

- 🔒 Google Alerts will give you a list of your keywords used anywhere on the internet.
- 🔒 Twilerts gives you a list of your keywords used on Twitter.

<29>

You will register on these two sites for a number of reasons. These alerts will give you content and inspiration for articles and status updates that you can post online. They will help to ensure that you know what's happening in your area. You can also use this information to write blog posts or film videos about your local area.

You also need these reports to assist you with brand protection. They will let you know if anyone has said anything about you, your staff or your company online. These alerts are EXTREMELY IMPORTANT. By knowing about any issues, you will be in a position to rectify any problems quickly.

Time is imperative online. Your reputation can be destroyed very quickly if you leave bad comments unattended.

What will make Google favour your website over every other site on the internet?

The answer is that Google have their own formula; it's called Google Algorithms.

Google's job is to direct their customer to the best site possible based on their enquiry. When the customer is searching for certain information or certain businesses, they want to give their customer what they are looking for, which is answers. They want to direct their customer to the most authentic website that offers the best information on a subject.

How will Google know who has the best information?

Google has algorithms, or a set of criteria, that rate websites in different ways. Websites will score extra points, and therefore preferential treatment, the more criteria they meet. So what things might they consider before they recommend your site?

<30>

Keywords

How to select keywords and key phrases

Keywords are the words that potential clients may use to find you. If you were searching for a Chinese restaurant in a local suburb, for example Melbourne, as a potential customer, you may type into Google 'Chinese Restaurant Melbourne'. Keywords are how Google knows what you are looking for. It's also how customers find you.

A large part of optimising your web pages is centred on how well you utilise specific keywords and phrases throughout your page content (as well as over your entire internet presence) and, of course, how relevant those words are to what people are searching for.

In real estate, our aim is to appear on page one of Google predominantly for topics relating to these keywords:

- 🔒 Your name
- 🔒 Your company name
- 🔒 Real estate agents (your suburb)
- 🔒 (Your suburb) real estate agents, plus any other identified keywords that potential clients may use.

- ☐ Check now to see if you are currently on page one of Google for '(your suburb) real estate' or '(your suburb) real estate agents'. This must be your aim. (In America this could be changed to the word 'Realtor' instead of 'real estate agent'.)

- ☐ While you are investigating in Google searches, check your own name. What shows first on page one for your name?

<31>

Please note: Keywords are critical to your overall online presence. Google has to know what you specialise in, in order to direct the appropriate traffic to your site. If you don't tell them what you do, they won't know.

People think that when you build a website and it goes live, others will find it. They won't.

Unless you have marketing strategies in place, you are leaving things in the lap of the gods.

As a consequence of keyword research across leading search engines and research tools with particular emphasis on Google, the following key search phrases have been identified for optimisation of each real estate landing page.

These are summarised below.

- ☐ You need to use your keywords on a consistent basis throughout your whole online marketing campaign.

Tip: Include your keywords at the very start and the very end of any of your articles, so that they flow naturally.

When Google assesses the relevancy of our pages, they **may** place emphasis on the words found in the first and last 100 characters of the text body in each page.

How do you know what keywords to use?

- ☐ Go to Google Free Keyword Planner: https://adwords.google.com/KeywordPlanner

Follow the prompts. It's very easy to use.

<32>

Here are some generic keywords and key phrases you can start searching:

- 🔒 (Your suburb) real estate
- 🔒 Real estate agents (your suburb)
- 🔒 Real estate agent (your suburb)
- 🔒 (Your real estate agency name) (your suburb)
- 🔒 (Surrounding suburbs) real estate
- 🔒 All of the staff in your office – their names
- 🔒 Houses for sale in (your suburb)
- 🔒 Homes for sale in (your suburb)
- 🔒 Apartments for sale in (your suburb)
- 🔒 (Your suburb) real estate for sale

Note: In different countries you may need to swap the words to suit; for example, in America you may need to change the words 'real estate agent' to 'realtor'.

Investigate through Google Keyword Planner how many searches happen in your area for the keywords mentioned above.

- ☐ If there are ten or more monthly searches for one topic, do a blog post on that particular topic. For example, if there are more than ten monthly searches for the keywords 'Real estate agents Adelaide' and you are located there, do an article about real estate agents in Adelaide.

- ☐ Use THOSE specific keywords for THAT particular article.

<33>

☐ If you are unsure how to use the keyword planner, just use some of the generic keywords listed above to start.

☐ As you put your content online, use your keywords throughout your entire online profile. That is, use the keywords appropriate to your article in your status update when you post it on Facebook, LinkedIn, Twitter, etc., and rename your photos with your keywords. (See below.)

☐ Search those terms on Google as well. Assess who shows up first – you or your competitor?

The keywords you use will need to be selected as a consequence of research conducted around your marketplace.

When you analyse your competitors as to where they rank on Google, if they are above you in the searches look for why that is.

Your keywords should only be applied to the relevant web pages on your site. Always repeat your keywords on your social media pages. Ideally, you should use different keywords for different pages on your site.

Placing keywords in the body of your page

You may place your keywords in several different places within the content of your web page, with varying degrees of impact on your Search Engine Optimisation results.

Outside of the general text on your page, the following may add further weight to your keywords when utilised as described.

Headings

Use headings on your blogs to create 'chunks' of information – be sure to include your key phrases and keywords in your headings.

<34>

Bold type

The fact that you put your key search phrase in **bold** in your text tells the search engine that you put emphasis on these words. Search engines may consider these phrases to be more important.

Of course, this also helps with visitors to your site being naturally drawn to specific parts of your page. The bold text increases readability and appeal.

Hyperlinks

You can create links to relevant articles and people. At the end of your article, for example, you can suggest another of your blog posts that's related to the one just read. You can also create links to social media profiles – both yours and other people's.

☐ Make sure any hyperlinks physically open in another window or page of your browser. If they don't, the person looking at your article will more than likely not come back to your website.

Note - Keyword stuffing is when you put TOO MANY keywords on your website and in the backend of your website. Google doesn't like you doing this.

Make sure that you don't upset Google.

Photos

When you take a photo with your phone or camera and you save the photo to your computer, it will normally aim to save the photo as a reference number; for example, it may save it as hlz67966k. It's just a whole lot of numbers and letters...

<35>

☐ From this moment on, rename your photos and videos with your keywords. Use the keywords that apply to that photo. For example, rename a photo of the bathroom in a property you're listing, adding the address and, of course, the name of your agency: '(Your suburb) - 3 Smith Street Bathroom Brisbane Real Estate Agents'. Then, when you upload these photos to your website, Google has something else to tie you to your keywords.

☐ This may also help you to appear in 'Google Images' for certain words. If you're not sure how to do this, right-click on your photo or video and click 'Save As' to your computer under a different name (rename the photo with your keywords). As another example, save your photo as '(Your name inserted here) Real Estate Agent Brisbane'.

☐ Use your keywords in the title of your blogs and in your social media pages. Use your keywords whenever it's relevant. Keep your message consistent. Google will also see that you have a consistent message across the internet on your chosen topics.

☐ Review keywords periodically, but start with the words suggested above so that we can begin to build on your profile for your service area.

Secret Agents ONLY drive traffic to THEIR website.

<36>

Drive Traffic to Your Site

Here is a list of potential websites that will assist you to build communities of raving fans. Use the following to first **ATTRACT** and then **DIVERT** traffic to your website.

- Real estate portals
- Online newsletters
- Opt-ins
- Blogs
- Facebook pages
- Facebook ads
- Online buyer alerts
- Direct mailouts
- YouTube
- LinkedIn
- Twitter
- Google Plus
- Snapchat
- Instagram
- Pinterest
- Google AdWords
- Email signatures diverting to your website
- Office database
- Podcasts

<37>

Work on Your Business

It's a fact: if you are not prospecting now for new business, you will not have a clear path of new listings in three months' time. What you do now will help sow the seeds of future business.

If you use intelligent online marketing methods, your website will effectively be prospecting for new business twenty-four hours a day. Your website will be your silent salesperson.

After you implement the methods suggested, it is anticipated that your visitor rate to your website will increase dramatically. Your conversion rate from enquiry to business client will also increase.

This will be evidenced by the number of subscriptions to your alerts/ newsletters and the number of direct enquiries that engage with you through social media, your networks and your accompanying online forms.

Then, of course, the ultimate measurement is the number of referrals, appraisals, listings and sales you will achieve as a result of your online marketing.

Websites

Remember that internet marketing has little benefit or purpose if potential clients arrive at your website and there is nothing to grab your visitors' attention.

If there is nothing of value that deals with their needs, or if it doesn't solve their problems, you will lose them. If you don't engage them, there will be no reason for them to return or recommend your site to other people.

<38>

Remember that the purpose of your landing pages is to engage visitors and get them thinking about you as their future real estate agent.

☐ If you are wondering what platform you should use for your website, I recommend **WordPress** or **Joomla.** They are easy to navigate and they are common platforms. Being a common platform makes it easier to have people work on them when the need arises. If you have a platform that is hard to use, you end up paying your web developer to learn how to use it. Save yourself a lot of time and money and employ someone who's an expert in that particular platform to begin with.

Secret Agents have specific strategies to get potential clients to visit their website.

Office Website

Strategies

The strategies that have been identified for generating new business opportunities through real estate websites include the following:

1. We have already analysed search engines whilst identifying popular search phrases related to real estate and we have **particularly focused on localised areas.**

<39>

2. We have focused on building sales and marketing funnels that will drive traffic to your real estate agency website.

3. We will be working on obtaining **links from other sites** to your website for selected keyword phrases.

4. Our aim is to always be on page one of Google organically for your keywords. Google Ads can be great; however, you still need to focus on strategies to get on page one organically (that is, not spending money in order to appear on page one).

So if your website is not there yet, I suggest you start with **Pay Per Click Ads** with **Google AdWords.** You can also include some Facebook ads.

Decide whether you are going to promote yourself and/or your company. You could also promote your properties for sale (if that is part of your marketing plan). You can employ someone to set up your ads on Google, but many people decide to set it up themselves. Ensure you set a small **daily budget;** that way it's impossible to spend over the amount you specify.

Always monitor your results! Depending on what area you are in and how many agents use Google AdWords, you may only need to spend a few dollars a day.

Many offices set a small daily budget; some offices only need to spend $200 a month. In my real estate office in a one-year period, we traced over $330,000 worth of available commission just from Google Ads. Remember to set a limit and don't get talked into big budgets. Test your results – monitor every day.

<40>

☐ Remember to always ask sellers WHY they called you. How did they find you? You must know EXACTLY where your leads are coming from.

When you are on page one of Google, this becomes a listing tool for you to help secure more listings. You are able to show and impress sellers that you are on page one. Show them that buyers will find you on page one of Google when they search 'real estate agents (your suburb)'.

If you are not on page one of Google, 'Pay Per Click' works incredibly well.

☐ Google AdWords - a specific, targeted Google AdWords campaign should be developed to support your internet marketing strategy. This campaign will focus on your selected key phrases and keywords, directing traffic to your landing pages. Trial and monitor.

☐ Investigate Facebook ads - trial and monitor

5. We will be making recommendations to improve your website structure, the design and overall attractiveness and the functionality of your site. These suggestions are offered in order to improve visitor conversion.

Mobile friendly

Make sure that your websites are **mobile friendly.** Some people choose to have a basic mobile site with links to their 'Contact Us', 'For Sale Properties', 'Sold Properties', 'About Us' and 'Testimonials' pages. A mobile site can include basic information and then have the option to divert to the full website.

<41>

Staff profiles on the office website

We will be covering your staff's personal online profiles in the next section. Firstly, what about their profiles on your office website?

☐ All staff should be included on the office website listed by their name. The office website should **also** have a complete individual page for each person. Generally, this would be under the section 'About Us'. It's here that each person can expand on all of their details with a full page under their name. You need to encourage your staff to constantly build on their profile and build on their online content.

On each salesperson's profile page, build their profile content with testimonial videos, videos of their sales and other relevant content.

Your aim is to help them build a massive online resume. Some agencies employ the services of a copywriter. If you need to get a copywriter, don't delay – get one.

On the profile page, you can include photos of sellers with Sold signs, written testimonials, and anything else to substantiate that your staff get results and they are the local experts. You can also do personalised bio videos.

The outcome is to try and be more personal and approachable to your clients.

☐ On the staff individual profile pages, you also need to use the selected keywords that apply to that person AND your area all the way through their profile pages. As an example, include their name, that they are an expert real estate agent in (your suburb) OR that they are the most experienced real estate agent in (your suburb). Talk about you, your suburb and real estate!

<42>

Remember, again to assist with Google, make sure all your photos and videos are named with your targeted keywords for the subject that you are talking about.

- ☐ Salespeople need to create a link from their email signature to their profile page or their own personal website. Make sure that on the link they send, there are some video testimonials on that page too. All salespeople need to be focused on building an online resume for themselves. When clients and potential clients click through and read their profile, it will substantiate their experience.

- ☐ Link any related content on other websites to your profile page or personal website. For example, when you post a video on YouTube put a link to your website back on the first line in the description on YouTube, diverting viewers to your personal website or profile page on the office website. Also include your details and contact telephone numbers. I've seen real estate agents produce a video that has gone VIRAL with no contact details on the video. Madness. Also make sure that your Facebook pages and other social media pages link back to your website as well. My personal Facebook page has a link to my Facebook business pages under the 'About' section.

- ☐ Make sure that on your business pages under the 'About' section you have links to your business website.

<43>

To recap:

Make sure your personal Facebook page has a link to your business Facebook page - you will organise this under the 'About' section.

And:

Make sure your business page has a link to your website under the 'About' section.

☐ Make sure that all your pages have links that connect on Facebook.

Individual Staff Profiles

Information for real estate principals

A lot of real estate agency principals are nervous about their staff engaging in self-promotion online. Don't be.

If your staff are building their online profile and linking their social media profiles to your office, they are helping you in lots of different ways. The biggest bonus is when they are getting listings and making sales as a result.

If they are building a profile where they can metaphorically be tied to your office on Google, this will help your company. If they are successful in attracting a huge following by promoting themselves attached to your agency, your office will benefit.

There will be lots of content online with their name **and** your name online. The more they build a profile with your agency, the harder it will be for them to consider leaving your office at a later date.

<44>

If your staff are getting known in the area, they are also helping YOUR office to become better known in the area. You want to help your staff by helping them build a big presence with regards to their personal profile on YOUR real estate agency website.

When someone Googles one of your team members, you want YOUR agency website to appear. Having a massive online profile will deter your sales staff from leaving the office they work in, especially if their profile is working for them.

Personal Branding: 'Your Website'

As you can see, in one way or another, all staff should have a website in their own personal name. Ideally, the aim is to have a massive personal profile on your OWN dedicated website. It's your resume that you can continually add to and improve. Your own personal website doesn't have to be anything expensive or complicated; it just needs to include your basic details.

There are a few ways that a staff member's website can be organised.

If you are the principal of an office and you are concerned about staff having their own website, you can set up a subdomain on the main real estate website. The domain name address would look something like this: johnsmith.yourcompanywebsite.com.au. It would be a separate website, but on the same server as your main business website.

The website would remain the property of the owner of the business. The owner of the business would generally pay for the setup and maintenance of the site (or as agreed), as it would remain the property of the office whilst the staff member is employed.

If the staff member leaves, the website would be removed from the internet.

I would suggest that if the office is paying for a personally branded website for the salesperson, that the only phone number on the website be the office phone number, not the salesperson's mobile number. If the office is paying for the site, the office should want every enquiry to come into one central location. This of course is to be negotiated between the parties.

In this scenario, should the office supply a website as a subdomain, the salesperson could also buy their own name as a full domain name and 'point' their domain name to the office subdomain website (this, again, would need to be in consultation with the office principal).

OR

The staff can buy and own their own domain names and create their own websites, such as www.theirname.com.au. This would generally be at the salesperson's cost. Under this arrangement, I would suggest that the salesperson own their website and they keep it should they leave the company.

I would recommend that the phone number that appears on the site be the office number; however, if the salesperson is paying for the site, this could be open to discussion (I am an advocate for every enquiry being directed to one central location at the office).

On leaving their place of employment, the salesperson would need to remove any company branding and any reference to the company. Some principals can get nervous about this arrangement, thinking that, if things turn sour with the employee, as the employer they would have no control over the site.

As office principal, assess your own situation and have clear agreements with staff regarding your online policies.

<46>

Naming

If you have a common name and you can't get your name as a domain name, you could get your name with other words attached – for example, include the words 'real estate' at the end: www.johnsmithrealestate.com.au.

Other possible options are www.thejohnsmith.com.au, www.yourjohnsmith.com.au, or www.johnsmithrealestatesuburb.com.au (i.e include your name and the area you operate). Just make sure you market and promote the full name of your site on all your marketing.

In Australia, protect your brand and always buy .com. AND .com.au domain names if you can (for your company and personally). The reason for that is because your competitor could buy the .com domain and forward it to their website (or anywhere else they choose). By doing this, they could effectively steal your traffic or damage your brand.

If funds are tight for your office or salespeople, each individual staff member could also buy their own domain name and point it to the main real estate agency website (I would suggest that they point it to their profile page and at least then they can promote their own domain name).

☐ Domain names - If you do not own your own name as a URL, buy it now. What I mean by that is, if you don't own www.yourname.com.au and www.yourname.com, buy them now!! For example, you can go to www.godaddy.com to buy domain names. They are moderately priced.

A personalised website will form the foundations of your online resume and profile.

<47>

Please note: If salespeople within an office choose to create their own website, the business owner would need to be consulted as there would have to be rules and guidelines - mainly concerning the office branding.

A real estate office should have a '**Social Media Policies and Guidelines**' book. This identifies what the office considers to be appropriate behaviour relating to social media and the individual office.

For a salesperson's individual website to be effective, they should have links to the company website, personal Facebook page, company Facebook page, Twitter page, LinkedIn page, and so on. Potential customers should be able to click the links on their website and be taken to Facebook or any other associated social media pages.

If the principal is opposed to the salespeople having their own individual profiles, then at least make sure that the agency principals have their own websites.

Why? You want people to find you on Google when they search the names of the real estate agents in your office. It further enhances your online profile and resume.

Social media sites are very beneficial as they can be associated and linked to other **authority sites.** The sites show who you are, what kind of following you have and who you are linked to. Google currently takes your social media presence seriously.

Secret Agents claim their domain name online before someone else does.

They don't risk THEIR name going to the competition.

<48>

Must-Have Content on Your Personal Website

This is about you!

As an example of a website, include the following as Topics or Tabs:

About Me – include all of your past experience and achievements. You can also have a video bio.

Video Testimonials - create a page on your website where you can put the embed codes from your YouTube channel. Add to your video testimonials continuously.

Your Listings - create a link from your website to your current listings for sale. Send people to YOUR real estate website, NOT a third-party website (never send traffic to the real estate portals - EVER!) You don't need to add properties to your personal site; a link will suffice. This website is about YOU. This is your online resume.

Your Sold Properties - have a link to the properties you have sold. Again, divert to YOUR real estate agency website, not to the real estate portals.

Suburb Profiles - have pages on your website where you review and write stories about all the suburbs in your area. Create a link from your Home Page that people can click on.

Contact Us - you MUST have a link to this on the Home Page. Make sure that customers can email you or phone you immediately. Make sure that visitors to your website can call you by pressing your phone number on their mobile phone or send an email by clicking on your email address.

Social Media Links - have links to all of the social media pages you have elected to join.

<49>

Websites - To Do List

Theme of your site

- ☐ **Company website** - The theme and the keywords used on the main page/Home Page of your company website should be about the company name and 'Real estate in (the suburbs you operate in)'.

- ☐ **For individual websites,** the theme and the keywords need to be about the salesperson's prospecting area/farm area and their name.

- ☐ **Include your phone number at the top of your website in the header.** Many people search for real estate agents on their smartphones. Your clients want the phone number to be accessible, EASY and FAST. Important point - again, make sure that your phone number can be clicked through from a mobile phone. If your phone number forms part of a graphic, users will not be able to click on it and call you. You will then be relying on them to find a pen, write your number down and then dial your number.

  It is in your best interest to make it as easy as you can for them to contact you. You want to cut out any steps you can. If it is too hard to call you, it could stop a potential client calling. With mobile phones being such a big part of our lives now, you need to make sure that you have this functionality.

<50>

☐ **Test your website on different devices.** For example, check your website on an iPhone, iPad, PC, Android, and so on. Test it on any devices you can. Check that the pages look the same everywhere and make sure the content appears correctly. Again, also check that when you land on a website page on your phone, you can click on a phone number and the number will dial.

☐ **Test your website in different web browsers.** Put your domain name into Internet Explorer, Google Chrome and Firefox to start with. Mac users, be sure to put the domain name into Safari. **Make sure it looks okay and it functions properly in all browsers.**

☐ **Install Google Analytics on your website.**

Secret Agents monitor EVERYTHING they do online:

They focus on results.

<51>

Google Analytics

I love this feature. I have an iPhone and I have the Google Analytics app. I love how I can check how many people visit my website on any given day. When I post a video or a blog post, I can see firsthand how well my article performed by tracking how many people visited my site. The app allows me to check my website traffic almost to the minute. It's extremely beneficial in business to know in an instant what's attracting attention. It helps to identify what's working and what's not.

Google Analytics will allow you to explore detailed information about where your customers live, the type of traffic that has visited your site and the visitor patterns exhibited. You will see where the traffic came from, what search engine it was directed from and, amongst other things, whether the visitor was referred by social media sites. This information can be used to assist with understanding how we can further improve different marketing aspects of your website.

Site Design Improvements

A number of recommendations we have made in regard to the design and structure of agency websites should be discussed with your web developer. Implementing these suggested changes should assist with your overall website effectiveness, performance and optimisation.

Some of these suggestions may have no bearing on your ranking in Google but are offered as tips to improve your ability to capture sales opportunity leads and convert visitors to sales. Discuss with your web developer about your particular website functionality.

<52>

Every company will have their website equipped with different software programs and applications. Obviously, it would be impossible to make specific recommendations for every single website without a detailed examination. We therefore can only make generic suggestions.

To achieve specific results, it may require you to engage a web developer to make changes to the source code of your pages. You may need to add plug-ins and make changes to other programs. If you are at all unsure, you should discuss the recommendations with your web developer.

Initiatives

In order to deliver the results from different strategies, a set of specific initiatives for websites has been identified that you can choose to implement. How you should implement these initiatives is explained through the following sections of the Internet Marketing Plan.

Secret Agents use specific keywords over their entire social media presence.

They know that's how their customers will find them.

<53>

List and last in real estate.

What are you doing to stand out from your competitors? What can you offer sellers that no other agent can? What's in your tool box? What are your listing tools? Listing tools are something you offer a seller as a bonus or incentive to list with you. It could also be a way that you substantiate you are better than the competition. Something that CAUSES a seller to list with you.

Part Three:
Using Technology & Social Media

How to use technology and the online world to your advantage

☐ You should use iPads, iPhones or tablets in your listing presentations. I'm not saying to use them for the entire presentation; however, you should use them to show your video testimonials, demonstrate your website and show sellers your contact management system. For example, you can show sellers how easily you may be able to sell their home. You can show them how many potential buyers you have on your database. You can also show that, should they list their property for sale with you, you have a number of buyers you could contact immediately, as soon as you have the paperwork to sell their home.

☐ Some agents take their iPad or tablet to open homes and send potential buyers a copy of the property contract and property information directly. It demonstrates their speed and efficiency.

☐ In listing presentations, you can also use your device as your accessories folder. Things that you would include among your accessories are items

<55>

like newspaper articles that substantiate your thoughts on the market. For example, you may want to demonstrate that it's a buyer's market, or a seller's market. You could have statistics about real estate prices in your area or newspaper articles with stories about what's happening in the market. You may have a list of properties that you have sold, and additional detailed information on those properties. You may have internal and external photos.

You could also have more information that sellers need to know; for example, how long the property took to sell, positives relating to the property and any negatives of the property. You can present this information beautifully on an iPad or similar device. You can have any information that is relevant forming part of your visual presentation; anything that will assist you in securing the listing.

My accessories folder when I started in real estate was a 20-page leather folder filled with newspaper clippings. Now our accessories folders can be interactive.

☐ Another way that you can use available technology is by sending text messages to let your clients know when something has been just listed or just been sold.

Always consider how technology can make you look efficient, free up your time and **how you can reach more people more easily and more cost effectively**. Consider how it can automate your follow-up and always think of ways it can help you to impress your clients.

<56>

Social Media

What is the REAL purpose of social media for business?

- [ ] Always remember that our main goal is to use social media to direct traffic to your site. Your website is always your main focus.

- [ ] You are building a community. You are connecting with friends who may use your services or refer you to their friends.

- [ ] To meet and engage with new potential clients and to allow people to get to know you.

- [ ] To build your brand over the internet.

- [ ] To help people find you on the internet and to assist you with Search Engine Optimisation.

Why do we have to be social?

They call it social networking for a reason: IT IS SOCIAL.

Social media for business is about strategic marketing. Social media will give you access to massive networking opportunities. Social networking will also provide you with the opportunity to include links to your website from reputable, high-ranking sources.

Do not underestimate the functionality and opportunities that come from using just some of these social networks in building your business. Explore them, understand them and then determine how you may be able to use them in the best way.

<57>

Where should you promote yourself as a real estate agent in your own name on social media?

Personally (in your own name) have a presence on:

Social Network	Home Page URL
☐ Facebook	www.facebook.com
☐ LinkedIn	www.linkedin.com
☐ Twitter	www.twitter.com
☐ YouTube	www.youtube.com
☐ Instagram	www.instagram.com

You should ensure that you have created a profile on each of the following social network sites.

Business - create pages for your business on:

- ☐ Facebook (business/like/fan page) - in the company name
- ☐ Facebook (you may choose to do a community page)
- ☐ Twitter - in the company name
- ☐ YouTube Channel - in the company name
- ☐ LinkedIn Business page (LinkedIn company page)

Secret Agents look for ways to create income and opportunities to build their business.

<58>

When a real estate office closes in their area, they ask the business owner if they would like to sell their phone number.

If an office has already closed they look at ways to retrieve the number.

Secret Agents look for easy wins.

Facebook

I want to make this clear: Your best way of generating leads through Facebook, especially at the start, is through your personal profile.

Connect on your Facebook personal page with people you know. Get to know local people through business and so on. These people will become listing leads and buyer leads. When you are building your database of friends on Facebook, think of the people you know from school, football, local business owners or friends you know through your children. Think of anyone you know and have good relations with. Remember that people are looking for conversations on Facebook.

Facebook business pages: the purpose of Facebook for business

Again, as with any social media platform, your aim is to drive people to your website. It's here that you will have your marketing funnel in place. You will then capture the details of prospective clients through your opt-in page and your buyer alert/newsletter.

Facebook tips:

- ☐ Get into the habit of posting something four times a day. Start at 7am and post something every four hours.

<59>

- ☐ Boost your most popular post at least once a week. Facebook will love you spending money and they will obviously reward you by showing your posts to a lot more people.

- ☐ Facebook loves people sharing content. Share one post from someone's page every day. Facebook will see that you are a helpful Facebook member.

- ☐ Re-post your best articles and photos. Go back through your blog posts and status updates and reuse!

- ☐ Tag relevant people into your posts.

- ☐ On your Facebook business page, make sure you use your keywords (Google will crawl your Facebook business page).

- ☐ One of the best examples of real estate agents doing social media well is **'The Corcoran Group'**. Search them online and follow them!

- ☐ For ease of posting, you can organise your Facebook status to go directly to Twitter. You can set that up by clicking here: **www.facebook.com/twitter**

There are a number of programs you can use to help you manage your social media platforms. They can help you to post your material on numerous sites at once. People are looking to learn something and to connect through Facebook business pages.

Facebook community pages

- ☐ Become active in your local area by starting a local community Facebook page and **make sure you make it about the community.**

<60>

Keep people up to date; use your community page to inform people about what's going on in the area.

- 🔒 Local events – kids' days out, fireworks, etc.
- 🔒 Get people to contribute concerning any Neighbourhood Watch issues
- 🔒 Discuss what the housing market is doing
- 🔒 Missing people
- 🔒 Lost dogs and cats
- 🔒 Lost personal effects
- 🔒 Anything that has the potential to affect the community
- 🔒 Local news
- 🔒 Information about local schools - what's happening?
- 🔒 Explain the demographics of your city or town
- 🔒 Discuss what's happening with the public transport system
- 🔒 The history of the area

Find other passionate local residents to join as admins:

- ☐ Design a community cover picture saying that the page was brought to them by you (or your company – do this discreetly; not a huge advertisement). Have a link to this page from your real estate website. Also have a link from this page to your personal website. Promote this page in your offline marketing.

<61>

Twitter tip

If you want to know whether someone is on Twitter, you can put their name into Google and then the word 'Twitter'. If they are on Twitter under their name, Google will return a search showing their 'handle.' Your Twitter handle is like your phone number. It lets people know where to find you.

You can also search for people within Twitter itself. You can search via their name or their handle; for example, my handle for my real estate training business is **@socialmediare.**

LinkedIn tip

For LinkedIn, I suggest you make posts individually on LinkedIn (if you want to, you can organise through LinkedIn that the updates you make there go directly to Twitter).

Google, at the moment, loves LinkedIn. LinkedIn has a very specific business focus and allows you to build your own network of business contacts, thus further consolidating your reputation. There are also some awesome strategies you can use with LinkedIn.

LinkedIn is AMAZING for Google search engines, as well attracting other agents to participate in business referrals.

☐ Create a business page as well as a personal profile. Always remember to use your keywords. Remember to complete your profile – build it out as much as you can.

People on LinkedIn are in a business frame of mind. When you make status updates, talk business with them.

<62>

What do you call your pages on social media?

The decision will be made easier depending on whether you are the principal of the agency or a salesperson.

Then assess your long-term plans. If you are the principal of a real estate business, you have two choices.

You can EITHER call your company pages by the name of the business (remembering that if you build your company's online profile, it will become an asset when you sell the business).

OR

You can choose to have your individual name as the profile name on all of your company pages. You must consider whether you want to build the company name or build your name.

Question - If you have your company YouTube account in your personal name, will you have all of your staff add their videos to your page or will you have them create their own channels? This is what you must consider. I would suggest having a business YouTube account. Again, you need to think about your future plans for the business.

For both pages in your description, identify and use the keywords based on the Google AdWords Keyword Planner.

- [ ] For business pages, make sure that you have your social media pages branded to your company by using your logo and so on (look at the rules of the social media sites relating to branding).

- [ ] Depending on the size of your office, principals could set up a number of community pages and have an agent in each of the farm areas control their appropriate pages. The principal would create the page under their profile and then make that

<63>

employee an admin. Staff should only make a few posts a day on this page. It should only take about 10 minutes a day to maintain. They could also get the help of a local area enthusiast.

☐ It would be the salesperson's job to update and market their page. If the office organises the page, the page would belong to the company should the employee leave.

☐ **If you are an individual or you are marketing yourself as an individual,** you can call your social media pages by your own name. These pages will remain your property (again, check with the office policy if you are an employee).

Please note: The beauty of having YOUR name is that it is less likely to change (unless you get married, divorced or you change your name by deed poll).

Whether you are an employee or a business owner, your place of business may change. Try to think carefully about what you intend to do in the future.

☐ Determine the right usernames and strive for consistent names across your social media presence.

Social Media Strategies

Don't forget, the purpose of using social media in business is to drive traffic to your website and increase your profile. The main ways to do this are:

🔒 Target local business owners

- 🔒 Establish and maintain community pages
- 🔒 Network with friends, and so on.

YouTube

Upload your video testimonials and market video updates to your company YouTube account. If you are a salesperson working in an office, talk to your agency principal regarding their thoughts. Some principals may not want you to upload the videos to your personal website. They may suggest that company videos are **their** intellectual property.

Again, so everyone's clear on what can and can't be done online, every real estate office should have a document on '**Social Media Policies and Guidelines'**. Devise your own guidelines in your office.

As always, make sure that you use your keywords - Remember that YouTube is the second biggest search engine in the world! Make sure you put links to your website from the description.

Mastering a social media site

Don't try to become an expert in mastering every single social media site. If you attempt to do this, you will never master any. It's important to just FOCUS on one or two and develop strategies for them. As a real estate salesperson, I would strongly suggest concentrating firstly on Facebook (to network and be social) and then focus on LinkedIn (for referrals and professional contacts).

Get a feel for what happens, watch what others do and say... Learn.

Also see where you have the best interaction and conversions and most importantly conversions!

Google Maps / Google+ Page

☐   Create a Google Maps page / Google+ Page

Optimise for your business. Your aim is to be on page one of Google when someone searches for real estate agents in your suburb.

To set up your page - www.google.com.au/business/

This is one of the quickest ways to get on page one of Google for your local area. You can do this yourself. Follow the prompts.

If you employ SEO companies, be careful of the costs. Engage someone who has a proven success history. Ask to see proof of their success and do your own research. Ask to see pages they have created for others that appear on page one of Google.

Niching Online

The power of niching online is that you can aim to **target** specifically **whoever or whatever** you want.

That is the beauty of Google and Facebook advertising. You don't have to advertise to the whole world. You can just promote to people who are searching with specific keywords – for example, someone who is specifically searching 'Houses For Sale Brisbane'.

With Facebook, you can specify even more. You can target groups specifically, such as females between 35 and 45 who live in certain suburbs of Brisbane.

You will become the expert

You need to become the expert and/or the reporter in your area. Eventually you will become both.

<66>

In other words, you will not only be reporting what's happening in your market from your point of view, but you will also be bringing to your customers information from other experts.

You will become known as the real estate agent with a comprehensive understanding of the market, an agent who has contacts with other experts and a professional who is serious about their knowledge of the area.

Fact: Your clients are searching online. You need to develop a massive online history. They are searching for information, they are searching for properties and they are searching for agents.

Other ways technology is being used in real estate

Drones / Unmanned aerial vehicles (UAVs)

Drone uses

Aerial footage – Drones are an amazing way to capture aerial footage of a property and the area that surrounds a home - they are also great for delivering sausages and pizzas... so I've heard?

Pre purchase inspections – Drones are also being used for pre purchase inspections for hard to see places - in particular roof inspections.

Energy efficiency – Thermal imaging cameras are being used to check a building's energy efficiency - For example to see if any heat is escaping from the roof cavity.

<67>

360 degree videos and virtual reality

Video technology now allows you to film 360 degree videos. This allows for a far more engaging and emotive video experience. Couple this with a virtual reality headset making it a fully immersive experience.

You can share 360 degree videos on social media channels including YouTube and Facebook.

Live videos on social media

You can connect with your audience live on social media channels showing them in real time what's happening in your business.

Secret Agents build a massive online profile.

Secret Agents know that their online profile is their online resume.

It could be how they are evaluated against their competition.

Part four:
Your Marketing Point of Difference

Positioning YOU as the Expert

You must claim your space as the expert agency in your area.

- 🔒 What niches are you going to focus on to begin with?
- 🔒 What suburbs or areas are you going to begin to market to online?

Here are some examples of where to start with topics for your articles:

- ☐ Local suburbs and areas
- ☐ Types of properties – apartments, semis, waterfronts; for example: (your suburb) apartments.
- ☐ Investors (in your suburbs)
- ☐ First home buyers (in your suburbs)
- ☐ You could also write about a local business in your area
- ☐ Your aim is for your website to become the authority site for your area.

<69>

The benefit of marketing online is that you can constantly run marketing campaigns in the background. Your aim is to position yourself as the real estate expert in your area.

Promote publicly that you are the expert in your area. Say it proudly. Potential customers will want your information, as you will have all the local real estate information in the one place.

Along the same lines, this is how effective marketing can be...

I bought hamburgers from a fish and chip shop once, purely because they had a sign out the front that said they had the best burgers in town.

I thought about it after my purchase. Their marketing worked. AND... they weren't the best burgers in town.

'Opt-Ins' – a.k.a. Lead Generators

Buyer alert / newsletter

What is your offer and strong call to action?

- ☐ You must set up an '**Opt-in**' on your office real estate website as a list builder/database creator.

- ☐ Make sure that your 'opt-in' is in the top right-hand corner of your site. This will be where buyers sign up to receive your buyer alert from your website.

- ☐ Once they register, they will be notified when new properties are listed for sale or for rent. If you don't currently have that functionality, have your web developer create buyer alerts that buyers can sign up to immediately.

<70>

Do it ASAP.

You can call your alert: (insert your real estate office name here) Buyer Alert

You can have your buyer alert sent out automatically, early every Wednesday morning. When determining when to send out your alerts, consider how big your office is and how many listings and sales you have.

Sending out buyer alerts once a week is sufficient for a small to medium office.

Your 'opt-in' will be your buyer alert and it will also double as your newsletter. On joining your VIP buyer alert, buyers will be advised when new properties are listed for sale on the market and when properties are sold.

This alert will also double as your newsletter. Your newsletter/buyer alert will feature information that you have sourced from articles written by local experts (more on that in a moment). Your alerts can also include local information and topics that they will find interesting.

- ☐ Remember, when you are on the phone to buyers or out with buyers or sellers, always obtain an individual's permission to add them to your weekly alert database. Make it a habit to ask every single potential client you deal with. Build your email database.

- ☐ In your newsletter, get creative. Have special offers from local businesses; for example, free coffee, free week at the gym, and so on. This is your chance to work with your networks.

<71>

☐ In your newsletters, you can promote special 'secret' places that residents might not know about. As an example, let people know about secluded beaches, bushwalks, cafes, picnic areas or waterways that only the locals or long-term local residents may know.

Your goal is to make the information relevant and interesting. It needs to be interesting enough that people will want to stay subscribed, and better still, they will want to share it with their friends.

☐ Be sure to place the 'opt-in' in a prominent place on your page (in the top right-hand corner of your page is usually an ideal position).

Having your buyer alert go out weekly will make you **focus** on what will be sent to your list of subscribers.

You will need fresh content to be sent out weekly. You will need new stock to promote. You will need price adjustments. You will need properties sold. You need fresh content to send out to your database! This will keep you focused on the task.

☐ On buyers signing up to your buyer alert, include your free report. As real estate agents, we have information that sellers and buyers want. We have property information and we have an abundant knowledge of our local area. If you are new in the area or you are new to real estate and you don't have that knowledge, your local experts can help you in that regard.

If you are organising your own personal website profile, with regards to your offer or opt-in content you can either have traffic directed to your company website 'buyer alert opt-in' or you can build your own email list with your own report (this would need to be in consultation with the office principal).

<72>

Now to create your report

The report will be sent to each person who opts in and leaves their email address. They can also download the report.

Great example titles for your report are:

- 🔒 7 Fatal Mistakes People Make When Buying and Selling in (Your Suburb)
- 🔒 7 Things You Must Know About Buying and Selling in (Your Suburb)

Test what works in your area. Tweak the title of the report if you are not getting a great response.

Tip: Don't necessarily change the content in your report; simply tweak the name of the report first. All areas are different, and therefore all of your marketing has to be tested and tweaked. What may work in one demographic may not work in another.

Other report titles you could test:

7 Ways to Make Money Buying Real Estate in (Your Suburb)

7 Ways to Get $15,000 More When You Sell Property in (Your Suburb)

7 Worst Mistakes People Make When Selling Property in (Your Suburb)

7 Ways to Get the Best Price When You Sell Property in (Your Suburb)

7 Ways to Save Money When You Buy in (Your Suburb)

7 Industry Experts Reveal All About Selling Property in (Your Suburb)

<73>

Tip: ask your market

Ask people what information they would like. You could also send out an online survey to people you know. Create a free survey at www.surveymonkey.com

Your report will be specific and relevant to your area, as every area has different things that affect their location. In it you can alert buyers and sellers to potential problems and issues they should be aware of regarding their property.

As examples, you could suggest they obtain further information on the following:

- Termites may be a huge problem in some areas
- Some areas may have mine subsidence
- Some properties may be affected by old systems title ownership, company title or leasebacks
- Properties may be on the water and have a jetty; what do buyers need to know?
- Some areas may be affected by fire
- Some areas may be affected by flood
- Some areas may have heritage listed properties
- Some properties may be under a flight path
- Let them know about the future of any new roads
- Advise them about the current infrastructure of the area
- Advise them about the zoning of the area
- Advise them about properties with energy ratings

<74>

🔒 Research any covenants in the area and make people aware they should consult with their local council

🔒 Suggest people research whether your area has faster internet speed on the way - is it coming? What internet connections are available?

🔒 If you are in a new area, you could suggest they make sure they have builder's insurance

🔒 If you are in an area where there are lots of apartments, suggest buyers get a strata report Suggest they also obtain a building inspection. Sometimes tenants don't report repairs and so on

🔒 Check swimming pool regulations

There may be things on the above list that buyers and sellers won't know about to research. Educate consumers on buying and selling in YOUR area. Your report doesn't have to be long. A couple of pages would suffice.

Remember, you are not giving legal advice. You are letting them know what to investigate and where they need to conduct their own due diligence.

The topics above can also be the subject of future blog posts.

Where do you market your buyer alert and the offer of your report?

☐ Market your offer through your social media pages

☐ On the Home Page of your website

☐ Have links to your report on your email signatures

☐ Promote the links to your report on all your marketing materials

☐ Promote your report both online and offline via paper newsletters, letters and brochures

Depending on how you have your buyer alerts set up, you may have autoresponders organised to communicate with your potential clients.

From your autoresponder, you can send out mass emails to your client list. A popular autoresponder is **Aweber**. When you send out emails from this program, they can be sequenced and automated.

Just remember, your website is where buyers and sellers will judge you. If your website is horrible, you will have a hard time getting online business.

Marketing Networks

Want to develop an online presence easily? And I mean easily....

Network with local experts

This is one of your online marketing strategies.

Have your local industry-related businesses write and contribute to your blog; that way YOU do not need to write a thing! They do all the work and all you need to do is post it onto your blog.

Local businesses will want to have the opportunity to promote themselves to your clients. You can, in turn, write for their websites.

Keep in mind, too, that a lot of local businesses won't have a website at all or they will only rate once on Google. So when you have other businesses' details online, as someone searches that company's name, YOUR company name will more than likely appear.

<76>

Network with and form alliances with local industry businesses

These businesses may have your customer **before** that customer comes to you or before they go to another real estate agent.

- ☐ Get to know local business owners in related industries. Arrange for them to meet in your office with the view that you will all be helping one another and referring business to each other. Some businesses may say no and that's okay. Move on to the next one in the same field that wants to increase their business.

- ☐ Ask your local experts for written articles that you can post on your site and send to your clients in your newsletter. You can then post links to your blog/newsletter on your social media pages and tag the other businesses and contacts into it. The key is that these businesses are local and they have a network of clients that you can share. You can help each other to build your business to a much higher level.

- ☐ Devise a plan to **actively market your website** via your local experts and local businesses. They are your networks.

Visit this link to see some video interviews that I filmed with local experts in about 2010 – www.buyingsellingahome.com

These videos were great in many, many ways. They helped me get known, they gave me great content, they gave me content to repurpose, they helped me get to know the local experts and they helped with my Search Engine Optimisation strategies.

<77>

If you decide you want to film videos with local business owners, once you've filmed the videos you will want to **repurpose the content for maximum exposure and benefit.**

Here are a few ways you can use the videos and also repurpose the content:

- 🔒 Give the expert a copy of their video
- 🔒 Supply them with a transcript of the video
- 🔒 You can each publish the video on your YouTube channels
- 🔒 Include the video (use the embed code from YouTube) and the transcript and put it as an article on both of your website blogs
- 🔒 Use this in your weekly newsletter/buyer alert
- 🔒 Upload the video onto both of your Facebook pages (both personal and business)
- 🔒 Tag your experts into the video
- 🔒 A few days later, include a link on your Facebook pages to their blog page with the transcript and video

It will depend on how much effort you want to put in and how much effort your experts want to go to as this is a lot of work. You might decide to start with written articles.

Example partners to network with are:

- ☐ Finance Broker
- ☐ Architect
- ☐ Building Inspector
- ☐ Removalist

<78>

- ☐ Storage Company
- ☐ Feng Shui Master
- ☐ Property Stylist
- ☐ Conveyancer
- ☐ Valuer
- ☐ Economist
- ☐ Property Journalist
- ☐ Local Businesses
- ☐ Solicitor
- ☐ Builder
- ☐ Landscaper
- ☐ Property Photographer
- ☐ Buyer's Agent
- ☐ Property Manager
- ☐ Local Celebrities

Article and press release contributions

- ☐ Ask local businesses if YOU could write articles for their websites. Remember, always think about how you can repurpose any of your content. If you write for other businesses, you can also repurpose your content on your site by including the article in your newsletter or blog.

Remember to use all of this as a listing tool. Show potential vendors your marketing strategies.

Building Your Profile with Videos

A while ago I read some statistics from America that said only 12 per cent of American real estate agents have YouTube accounts. In these same statistics, it says that 73 per cent of homeowners said they would choose an agent using video over one that didn't.

Don't underestimate video - it is a very powerful product.

☐ Always obtain video testimonials from past buyers and sellers. Ask some of your previous raving fans from over the years. Write a list of as many past buyers and sellers as you can. Make it a goal to contact one person a day to ask for a video testimonial about your services. Get as many videos as you can. You can also film videos of yourself giving information about past sales, what the property was like, how long it took to sell, what features the buyers liked, and so on. You can film these on your mobile phone. Testimonials do not have to be elaborate or be to a professional standard; just make sure that the lighting and sound are great.

☐ Have a professional company video both you and your office, showing your business and location. It has to be short, sharp and to the point.

☐ Film videos highlighting local suburb profiles. Demonstrate that you're the expert in your area. You will also be building relevant information onto your site for Google.

<80>

- ☐ Do articles and videos on what it's like to live in YOUR area. Tell potential buyers what it's like to live where you are. Tell them about the schools, shops, parks, gyms, coffee shops, beaches, and so on.

- ☐ Tell buyers why they will want to live in your area. What's good about it?

- ☐ Do quick videos or articles letting people know about interesting things that are happening in your community.

- ☐ Use only professional quality video clips on your Home Page; otherwise, you run the risk of not conveying the right sort of branding for your business or products. First impressions are everything. Videos can say so much more than your visitors can ever read and are therefore an extremely powerful communication source. If you are talking only, the clip should ideally be under two minutes.

Place other videos throughout your site on other key landing pages.

The Real Estate Marketing Academy Online Course includes a whole course designed to teach you how to use video marketing in your business. For more information please go to www.realestatemarketingacademy.com.au.

<81>

What is Your USP and How do You Show Clear Positioning?

Video is an easy way to stand out from the crowd and it's an easy way to have a clear USP.

By using videos and social media correctly, it demonstrates that you are locally focused and clearly involved in the community online. Videos will allow you to become known very, very quickly.

Unique Selling Propositions should be a significant aspect of marketing in any business.

Whilst people place a lot of emphasis on having a USP for their business, we really should have consideration to such a statement for each of your landing pages on your websites as well.

You can house your videos on a number of video sites, including YouTube and Vimeo. For the purposes of what we want to achieve as real estate agents, we will use YouTube.

Blogs

We mentioned blogs earlier, but now let's consider them in more detail.

Blogging should absolutely be a part of your online marketing strategy. However, many agents find it difficult, quoting both a lack of time and the struggle to come up with a continual supply of interesting topics. There is a simple way to get over your fear and get on with the job.

<82>

Let's get clear: what is blogging?

Let's just say for ease of understanding and for the purpose of this story that blogging is really just a fancy name for writing an article about a chosen subject on your website.

The term originated from the words 'web log'. Web log means an article 'logged' or recorded on the web, or internet. A blog is essentially your personal electronic magazine. It's a collection of articles written by yourself and other authorised contributors.

Blogging can easily be a part of your overall internet marketing strategy and can assist with many things such as:

- 🔒 Giving valuable information to your customers.

- 🔒 Getting your name on page one of Google so that your potential customers can find you (if you're not on page one of Google your potential customers may not know you exist).

- 🔒 Positioning yourself and your real estate office as the experts in your area or niche.

Network with local business owners; communicate normally and then keep in touch via social media. As suggested previously, ask related local business owners to provide you with articles to add content to your site. Your experts have local area knowledge AND they have local area networks. Your aim is to find people to form alliances with, whereby you can cross-promote each other's businesses.

<83>

Where can you get inspiration for the subject material?

That's easy! If you haven't already, open up your browser and go to Google and type in these words: 'Google Alert'. Follow the prompts and sign up. Once you have an account, you can start to create alerts.

Google scans the internet every day to look for any new articles with certain words in the content, and when they find something they will deliver it straight to your inbox.

What this means is you can set up a Google Alert for your suburb, your industry, and so on. For example, if you are located in Perth, set up separate alerts for Perth real estate, Perth and suburbs you cover in Perth. You might also like to include some influential people you follow; people who comment on the topic of real estate in Australia.

This will give you fresh content about your area and your profession every single day. Say, for example, that a real estate expert commented that the market was slow, yet your office had made more sales that month than ever before; you could write a blog discussing their opinion and then give your own views.

You might also receive a Google Alert letting you know that your local council is planning something that you either agree with or do not agree with. You could write a blog about that. Don't plagiarise their words; you will simply be referencing and discussing what they have written. It's a great start when you have a topic that you feel strongly about.

Blog articles are easy to create (less than 10 minutes if you keep it simple), they are free, and best of all, they are search-engine friendly.

Remember, your content needs to be relevant. There is no point in talking about anything other than what you are positioning yourself to be the expert in. Your aim should be to become the expert in your area and niche.

<84>

Now that you have a steady resource centre for content, you need a strategy. One of your strategies involves your local area networks.

Blog planning

Next, you need to develop an online marketing plan.

- ☐ Map out a 12-month calendar, January through to December.

- ☐ Ask each of your industry experts to contribute something relevant and interesting to your blog and schedule them in your diary. If your buyer alert goes out once a week, you could include an article from one of your experts every second week.

- ☐ Think about what's happening throughout the year. For example, we know that there is Easter, spring and Christmas. You can decide what you are going to write about for those months well in advance.

Other things you can choose to write about in your blog:

- ☐ Suburbs in your area

- ☐ Properties for sale in your area, for example (your suburb) houses for sale

- ☐ A niche, such as waterfronts or apartments

- ☐ Local businesses in your area

- ☐ (Your suburb) real estate agents. Write a blog post about your office.

- ☐ (Your suburb) property management. Write a blog post about your property management department

- ☐ (Your suburb) rentals. Write a blog post that your landlords will find interesting

<85>

☐ Ask local industry-related businesses to contribute to your blog; that way you do not need to write a thing! They do all the work. All you need to do is post it onto your blog.

You can do blogs about those topics, therefore, representing different niches and different keywords.

Remember that anything you put online in your marketing efforts stays online. The more content you add, the more the content builds up; think of the compounding effect and the momentum that this will achieve for your company.

You should aim to write blog posts at least once every week. Remember, obtain content from your networks – it will be so much easier.

Once you have your completed article, put it on your website and include links to Facebook, LinkedIn, Twitter and any other social media sites you have. Make sure your articles are RELEVANT and interesting. The best idea is to network normally and approach local business owners with the aim of helping each other and your networks.

It's important to select the right people. Let them know that your intentions are to help them to promote their business through your combined networks.

Once you have their trust, obtain their permission to 'friend' them on Facebook. Then, at APPROPRIATE times, you can comment, like and share their material, as they will hopefully do with yours.

Don't be pushy. Don't try to peddle your wares on their page. You are getting to know their friends and they are getting to know you. Don't spam their page with your business. That's not what social media is about.

Again, the critical point to remember with blogging is that you need to write articles that are interesting, that other people will want to read and then want to share. Within these articles include links to

<86>

other pages on your site with relevant topics. Remember, teach people something they don't know. Teach people something that will help them, and help others.

Your blog must be good for Google, as well as your potential reader.

You've no doubt read that you need to make your blog post titles 'search-engine friendly', but doing so often kills the creativity and the initial appeal of your article.

When you publish your blog post, follow this advice:

Think like a sharp-thinking journalist. Think about catchy lead-in headlines when you are promoting your blog on social media. Make your lead-in headlines or titles to your story interesting. You might choose to ask a question, share the lead-in to the story or offer an interesting title that gets your reader's attention.

Keep it short and simple. If you make your initial post title too long, you run the risk that you'll either confuse the reader or give them too much information, then there's no need to read the post itself. The trick is to entice your reader with the lead-in and the headline.

In stage one, your goal is to appeal to the initial readers that will likely view the post on the day that you publish it. But what happens after your post is relegated to the archives? It's unlikely someone will spend hours just browsing through your archived posts.

Instead, they'll likely discover your 'great content' via one of the search engines. That's where your focus needs to be.

With this in mind, you need to make your post's TITLE and everything else relative. Make sure you have an effective use of keywords so that it can benefit you in Google's search results.

<87>

Tip: When possible, write stories that relate to current issues which are already of interest in the media. Reference and hyperlink those articles in your article as well.

☐ **Register on Sourcebottle (in Australia): www.sourcebottle.com.** This is where journalists source content for stories they are working on. You might be able to get yourself some free PR.

Commenting on other blogs

Commenting on other industry-related blogs can help you in number of ways.

This can be a useful initiative for further developing your credibility and it can help associate you with other authority websites.

It can also assist you to build a bigger presence online with positive content (always make comments helpful and balanced, as you want your comments to work for you, not against you).

Blogs for your profile

In your blogs, use your keywords for separate subjects in separate articles. For example, '(your suburb) real estate agents' would be one article.

If that is, say, 'Aspley real estate agents', then after that you could write an article on 'Brisbane real estate agents'.

☐ In your blogs, use hyperlinks to other articles that you have written that are relevant. Also make sure that you have links to your social media profiles and

<88>

so on. Don't go overboard with 'keyword stuffing'. Just use the right amount of words so that it makes sense and so that it's appropriate for the article.

Podcasts

Podcasts are a fantastic way for real estate agents to build a MASSIVE online profile. Having your own podcast show, will assist to position you as the expert, helping you to build credibility and to become the authority in your area.

Podcasts easily allow you to repurpose material to help with being found on page one of Google.

How do you get started with a podcast? And how do you repurpose material?

- You initially write the script of your podcast and this becomes your transcript to display.

- You record yourself talking through it....

- We have your audio converted to a podcast syndicated to several podcast stations - apps like itunes, stitcher and overcast.

- Your podcast can be displayed on your website.

- Your podcast can be distributed to all your social media channels.

- We can also create a video from your audio to load onto YouTube and social media.

Google loves fresh content and doing podcasts enable you to produce your content in many formats.

<89>

Tip: Reuse your material, and reuse it any way you can.

Examples:

- [ ] For any videos that you film, upload the video to your channel on YouTube.
- [ ] Upload your video to Facebook. Don't just post the link; upload the video. The video will stay on your Facebook page and it will be available when your potential clients begin to research about you.
- [ ] Write a blog post and include the embed code in your blog.
- [ ] Transcribe your video into words.
- [ ] Give your industry experts videos and transcripts to put on their websites.
- [ ] Lastly, use your social media platforms to promote links to your new material.

Tip: If your existing website doesn't have the functionality to have a blog or podcast, instead of replacing the whole website, you might choose to add these to your website.

All you need to do is buy a domain name or create a sub-domain and create another site suitable for your blog/podcast. Put a tab on the Home Page of your existing site that says 'Blog' or "Podcast". You will then divert traffic to your new pages.

Links to Your Website

Links could be one of the most significant factors in achieving the best ranking on Google.

<90>

You will obtain links that divert back to your website from sites that are relevant to your own website theme and subject matter. You will obtain plenty of links from your network of industry experts by posting your content on their sites. They will reference you and your site. You will also post their material and links to their sites.

Remember that, as far as Google goes, you are who you hang out with online. The credibility and reputation of your website is critical to the search engines ranking you well in search results. Don't engage in spam behaviour.

Another excellent source of link building is through adding content to other sites yourself. The most common practice is creating your own blog and writing articles to be published on the internet through your website. You may find some value in contributing to other blogs or forums. You can also comment on other industry articles.

Social media shares, likes and comments can also give you credibility with Google.

Think about your marketing funnel.

- 🔒 Attract potential customers via multiple sources
- 🔒 Collect their details
- 🔒 Make sure that you keep in contact with them.

Secret Agents know that their online profile is their own personal advertisement that runs 24 hours a day. They also know it's free.

<91>

How do you Monitor the Effectiveness of your Online Marketing?

A set of performance criteria (key performance indicators) should be identified for your website indicating the level of traffic and business revenue that's attributable to your website. These KPIs should be taken prior to implementation of your marketing plan; they should be monitored on a regular basis and analysed at regular reviews.

KPI: Description of measurement

How do you measure what's working for you online?

- How many people contact you to appraise their property as a result of your marketing online via social media, Google Ads, SEO strategies, and so on?

- How many visitors go to your website? Monitor this through your **Google Analytics** program.

- How many people opt-in to your newsletter/buyer alert report?

- How many friends/followers/likes and connections are on your social media pages?

- How much interaction is happening on your pages – how many shares, what is your reach?

- Then the ultimate test, of course, is to measure how many listings and sales you are securing.

Secret Agents always think about their why – They know their purpose.

<92>

Checklist Recap

To do:

- [ ] **Register for Google Alerts and Twilerts.** They will inspire, give you knowledge and help you with your brand protection.

- [ ] Register for Sourcebottle for free PR opportunities.

- [ ] Identify keywords that you should be using throughout your marketing.

- [ ] **Improve your personal online presence on your company website.** Include the keywords that we have identified. Include photos and videos (remember to rename them with your keywords). Put links from your social media pages through to your website. Tie them all in together.

- [ ] **Build content onto your Facebook 'like' business page.** Upload photos (renamed). You can add staff photos, location photos, and so on. Remember to use your keywords in status updates on your business page. You also may like to start a community page.

- [ ] Set up Facebook.

- [ ] Set up Twitter.

- [ ] Set up LinkedIn.

- [ ] Set up YouTube.

- [ ] Set up Instagram.

<93>

- [ ] Put links to your social media pages on your website.

- [ ] **Use videos.** Prepare a list of past sellers and buyers who you think would be happy to give you a video testimonial. Arrange a time to film them. It doesn't matter how long ago you sold to them or sold for them.

- [ ] **If you are a salesperson, put your testimonials on your own YouTube channel.** Make sure you use the right keywords and so on, then embed the videos onto your website.

- [ ] Make sure you have a link back to your website on the first line of your description on YouTube. Include your name and your phone number.

- [ ] **Use these videos on your iPhone, iPad and website.** Show these videos to prospective sellers, and so on.

- [ ] **Upload videos to your social media business page.** Put links on your social media pages as well as to your blogs.

- [ ] Organise a buyer alert 'opt-in' on your website.

- [ ] **Put together a report,** for example '7 things buyers and sellers should know about buying and selling in (your suburb)'. Include this as part of your buyer alert.

- [ ] **Have the opt-in on your website in the top right-hand corner**. This is where you will build your list of clients you can market to.

<94>

☐ Identify some local reputable business owners you can work with to network and refer clients to. This could be architects, interior designers, building inspectors, removalists, property photographers and so on, as listed above.

   ☐ Have a meeting with these business owners in your office and explain the local networking opportunities. Join with them on social media. Ask them to contribute to your newsletters, and so on. If they will do a video for you, even better. Think of how you will be able to tap into the local networks on social media, their clients and their friends.

   ☐ Ask your local experts to contribute to your blog.

   ☐ Organise a marketing calendar - plan a date when articles are due from each expert.

☐ **Build a marketing strategy to network with your experts.** They could have access to your potential clients.

☐ **Have a link from all of your email signatures to your individual profile pages.** Build on this page, as this is your online resume. Buyers and sellers who receive your emails will click on it. You will take them to your page with your online resume.

☐ **Have your personal profile website in your own name.**

<95>

☐ Register it under your individual names, for example, www.lisab.com.au. The idea is to build a lot of content about YOU. It will help people find you. It's impressive and it substantiates what you have achieved. Buy personalised domain names, yourname.com and yourname.com.au (buy both the .com. and the .com.au). Everyone must have a personal website in their own name. This is where you build your online resume.

☐ If you are the principal of a business, you can elect to have the domain name for your company then have subdomains for all your agents.

☐ If it is set up as subdomains, I would suggest that staff buy their domain names and point them to the subdomain website.

☐ **Personally** set up a Facebook personal page, LinkedIn, Google+ and anything else you want, but focus mostly on just one or two.

Don't be a master of none.

☐ **Set up pages for business** on LinkedIn, Facebook, Twitter, Instagram and YouTube.

☐ **Organise Pay Per Click ads.** Organise Google first and then Facebook. Set budgets and test.

☐ **Organise local suburb profile pages using your keywords.** You can Google about the area - research the area and write brief articles. You can also do a talking video. Tell people what it's like to really live in your area.

<96>

- ☐ **Organise Google Analytics on your website.**
  Download the app on your phone, then you can see how much traffic you are getting on a daily basis.

- ☐ **Have your Google+ page or Google Map optimised.**
  You should be on page one of Google with your map when you type in real estate (in your suburb).

- ☐ **Have a video on your Home Page on your website**.
  Don't have it any longer than about one minute to an absolute maximum of two minutes and preferably have a company introduction, or personal introduction if it is a personal website.

Secret Agents track all of their successful conversions.

<97>

www.TheRealEstateHotline.com.au

Real Estate Coaching On Demand

Coaching

Accountability

Resources

Systems

Strategies

Framework

Support

Part five:
Video Marketing

I love video marketing. Without a doubt, it is the quickest way to become known in your area. Video marketing can help you obtain exposure for yourself and your office. Videos can give you a massive point of difference over your competitors and you can also use video as a way to prospect for new business.

Let's look at 24 ways to use video in your real estate business

1. Video testimonials

Your aim is to have a large number of video testimonials on your website. Upload your testimonials to your social media pages and YouTube – then include them on your blogs and your website.

When you are with potential clients you can show them your videos via your smartphone, tablet or computer. You can also send them the video, or send them a link to a page on your website that houses all of your video testimonials.

Gone are the days of presenting handwritten and often misspelled testimonials to clients.

Video testimonials create impact – simply because clients can see and hear REAL people. You don't have to rely upon your potential client believing (or not believing) that your written testimonials are genuine.

<99>

Benefits to you and your agency

🔒 Video testimonials give your business 'social proof' and legitimacy. The benefit of a video testimonial is that you are not saying how good you are; other people are doing it for you. There is another major benefit when you upload your video testimonial to YouTube and other video websites – you will also gain the benefit of automatically supporting your Search Engine Optimisation strategies. The more good content you have online, the better.

🔒 Video testimonials provide excellent evidence that you have not only created enough rapport with your prior client, but you have obviously provided an excellent service.

An additional use for your video testimonials

You can also upload your video testimonials and company video to your office iPod and have the audio playing when customers ring and they are placed on hold. There are obvious benefits - you have something about your company playing to a captive audience and you are again letting potential buyers and sellers hear what your customers have to say about you.

It's easy once you know how to request, produce and film videos. Don't think about getting video testimonials. Just do it.

2. Use technology to support your listing presentation

Use iPhones, iPads, iPods or other smartphones and tablets to show a selection of videos to your prospective sellers during presentations.

<100>

You can even demonstrate on video exactly how your website works, or what their property would look like on YouTube or on a third-party website.

Benefits to you and your agency

Ultimately, your iPad or smartphone becomes your 'accessories folder'; it is here that you can provide evidence to support your methods, your knowledge, your customer base and your reputation. You can easily stand out from your competition.

Secret Agents create and follow checklists and blueprints.

3. Montage videos

You can use montage videos to showcase your properties for sale, not only on your website but on other third-party real estate websites.

Also... If you want to impress a seller whilst at a listing presentation, take photos of the property as you do the tour of the property. Quickly produce a montage video on your phone before you leave the appointment. It's easy to impress.

Benefits to you and your agency

You can use these property videos to either add value to your marketing package (at no cost to the vendor) or you can choose to upsell to the property owner at a small cost. I prefer to add value and win the listing. These videos are cheap and very easy to do.

<101>

4. Allowing people to 'opt in' from your website

You MUST have a buyer alert on your website. Your buyers want to know when a property becomes available to buy. This 'opt-in' facility on your website will attract your target market. This is also how you build your online business.

Your aim is to collect a database of buyers. As part of this process, you should ALSO include video presentations, testimonials and other news. When sellers 'opt in' for your report, you can provide a link to a series of videos tailored to them.

Benefits to you and your agency

- You will contact buyers with properties for sale; you will make sales
- If your content is interesting, people will stay connected to you even if they have already bought or sold
- You are providing valuable content to your clients (your target market)
- You are positioning yourself as the expert
- You are building affiliations within your own and related industry groups
- Your network group can also cross-promote your videos
- The information you're providing may go 'viral' through the use of social media
- You are creating a database
- You are also adding to your list of potential sellers and buyers

<102>

5. Videos delivered with an introduction letter

Videos can also be professionally packaged and hand-delivered to your potential client, either by providing a hard copy via DVD or online via a digital file. These videos may include your company video, client testimonials, frequently asked questions, properties for sale or anything you want.

You can also create an online magazine that incorporates in one easy-to-access place all your latest videos and reports.

Benefits to you and your agency

This highlights your point of difference:

- Shows that you are a business with an innovative approach
- Shows you can add value and provide a unique customer experience
- Provides a means by which you can strengthen your reputation as an industry expert
- Exposes your potential client to your innovative methods for marketing their property

There are plenty of ways you can prepare, package and market these videos.

6. Using videos to market your business through social media

Social media is used for many reasons, but one of the distinct advantages of this technology is the opportunity for us to use video marketing to promote our business and our properties for sale to a diverse audience.

<103>

Benefits to you and your agency

Social media can help you improve your search engine ranking considerably, which means more people visiting your website and more potential clients. You always have the chance for your video to go viral.

Sites such as Facebook, Twitter, LinkedIn and personal blogs can define your media presence and ensure your business name is 'top of mind' for your audience.

7. Local area videos

Local area videos will highlight your knowledge of the area, while also providing useful and essential information for your prospective clients.

Benefits to you and your agency

Benefits include:

- 🔒 Confirmation that you are THE expert in your area
- 🔒 The videos will be of great benefit to potential clients, adding value
- 🔒 An opportunity to market your business within the context of your local area and other businesses within the area
- 🔒 Assisting in Search Engine Optimisation for your website

8. Create your YouTube channel to showcase your videos

Include all of your videos in the one place. Don't give your cameraman the views or hits on their YouTube channel. Upload all of your public videos to YOUR channel on YouTube.

Tell your clients that their property will be advertised on YouTube with a worldwide audience.

Benefits to you and your agency

Showcasing your videos on the internet provides the following advantages:

- 🔒 All of your past videos will be housed in the one place
- 🔒 The opportunity to position yourself as an expert, not only in your field but also in marketing and innovation
- 🔒 A point of difference
- 🔒 Search Engine Optimisation efficiencies
- 🔒 Evidence of your marketing expertise
- 🔒 Your history and proof of your results

9. Campaigns

A video campaign is an excellent way to market your services and gain ongoing interest in your business.

By producing a series of videos that are related in content or are produced as part of a series, customers are more likely to keep coming back, helping to create a 'top of mind' awareness for your business. For example, produce a video of the history of your local area. You could also video an investor series of videos or a buyer series of videos.

A completely different way of doing this is like AAMI did – Google the ads they did with Ketut and Rhonda.

Identify niche markets or other groups common to your area. Always run niched marketing campaigns in the background to your other more generalised marketing.

<105>

Benefits to you and your agency

- 🔒 A point of difference
- 🔒 Search Engine Optimisation efficiencies
- 🔒 These campaigns zero in on people who may not have found you otherwise
- 🔒 A video campaign or video series may be uploaded on a website with no maintenance required

10. TV – Reception video

Setting up a flat screen TV in your reception area or in other prime locations (for example, high footfall or high 'waiting time' shops such as sit-down cafes, doctor's surgeries, takeaway restaurants, car washes and so on) can provide enormous opportunities to market yourself, your listed properties and your business. Display videos produced by you of the local area; don't just sell you. Provide interesting information.

When you take advantage of this method, you will reap benefits linking targeted campaigns to your captive audience.

Benefits to you and your agency

Benefits include:

- 🔒 Showcasing your business while people wait and watch
- 🔒 Top of mind awareness (they see your marketing everywhere)
- 🔒 A passive approach to marketing where your video isn't simply 'just there' but providing interest

<106>

11. Gifts to clients

Videos can make a wonderful gift to clients or prospective clients: upon completing a sale, for their birthday or just to show you care. Buyers can take any of their friends and family worldwide on a virtual tour of their new property, or sellers can use it as a keepsake to reminisce about their past home.

Benefits to you and your agency

- Creation of a memento to keep
- Addition of value for your client
- A point of difference for your business
- It helps to create the 'wow' factor
- It's extremely low cost
- It has your name on it forever

12. Seasonal videos

Videos can be created to market special events, such as Christmas, Easter or the Melbourne Cup. A video can be made about anything topical. Get creative. Get clever.

Benefits to you and your agency

As well as adding value, add the 'wow' factor:

- Positive engagement: you have a reason to contact past and prospective clients
- It can get people talking
- If your video is clever, different or has special flair, it may even go viral.

<107>

13. Videos of Frequently Asked Questions (FAQs)

Create and promote a series of **Frequently Asked Questions** on video and display them on your website. An example could be: What are the best tips for selling my property? Videos will help to provide practical help and answer any questions people may have. Most of the time, people will favour the option of having something that they can view at their leisure.

Benefits to you and your agency

Benefits include:

- 🔒 You are seen and acknowledged as the expert
- 🔒 If you do a great job, your video could go viral
- 🔒 There is consistency in information and you are adding value to your clients

14. Creating videos just for buyers

Video has the advantage of being used extensively in television and movies to not only entertain, but to create a bond and emotional impact with the audience.

By having videos on your website aimed specifically at buyers, you not only provide information on your business and on properties you have for sale, tips on buying, a history of the area and what they need to know about the area, but you can help them with the whole buying process. You can also help establish a more personal approach and stronger rapport than you might otherwise have.

One side benefit of providing videos to buyers is that sellers themselves can see how your business attracts and values buyers.

Benefits to you and your agency

Benefits include:

<108>

- A separate and targeted channel for communication directly to buyers
- An opportunity to market to buyers and sellers
- Another opportunity to create 'top of mind' awareness

15. Creating videos just for sellers

Like creating videos for buyers, doing the same for sellers can create an excellent impression and help establish rapport – this is, of course, in addition to the useful information you provide them with in your presentation.

You can film information videos relating to particular questions sellers may have. You could answer questions on the subject of commission, auctions, franchises and so on.

Benefits to you and your agency

Benefits include:

- A separate and targeted channel for communication directly to sellers
- Another opportunity to create 'top of mind' awareness
- Another opportunity to increase your Search Engine Optimisation ranking
- You are helping sellers find answers

<109>

16. Staff profiles

A video that introduces your business and your staff can be an excellent marketing tool if done properly. Not only will buyers and sellers feel more comfortable if they can see the face behind the name (as well as any other information you may wish to share), it also improves Search Engine Optimisation results by having the names of your individual staff included in the video description.

Benefits to you and your agency

- Helps you create instant rapport
- Introduces your team to the world
- Promotes the feel that your staff are long-term employees
- Another opportunity to increase your Search Engine Optimisation

17. Direct prospecting video

A direct prospecting video is used, for example, if you are targeting a certain property for a buyer. If a buyer has asked you to see whether the owners would consider selling, you can then deliver a video directly to the occupant of the property asking them the question. You can ask them to pass the video on to their neighbours if they don't wish to sell.

Benefits to you and your agency

- It is targeted and personalised
- Shows heightened professionalism by demonstrating that your business can provide such a product and tailor it to that individual or property

<110>

🔒 Emphasises a point of difference between your
business and other businesses

18. Video signatures on emails

It is surprising that more businesses do not take advantage of this
simple yet effective marketing tool. Consider how many emails you
or your business send out in a week – and now think! Every one of
those emails could include a photo with a play button on it (so it
looks like a video) with a hyperlink to a video. The video could be of
individuals, testimonials, one of your videos that has thousands of
hits, your business or your local area.

Benefits to you and your agency

🔒 It is a high-frequency means of marketing

🔒 It is a passive form of marketing where the
individual can choose to view the video

🔒 Emails are often forwarded on, increasing your
exposure

🔒 You direct what content is there

19. Follow up on appraisals

After attending an appraisal and hopefully promoting your points of
difference and your innovative marketing methods, one of the most
memorable and effective things you can do is provide a personalised
video email to say 'thank you'.

Do not underestimate the impact that this can have upon a potential
client or upon someone you have just recently signed up as a client.

Benefits to you and your agency

Benefits include:

- 🔒 It is a real point of difference
- 🔒 It creates a 'wow' factor
- 🔒 It is something that is often talked about to friends and family after it is received and leads to new business

20. Company profile video presentation

We have all been victim to having to sit through a company video that is either sleep-inducing, stilted, poorly presented – or just plain embarrassing.

You need to plan and design a professional company profile video as well as engage the services of a professional videographer and production company to produce a high quality product.

Benefits to you and your agency

- 🔒 You will have a video to be proud of
- 🔒 The video will highlight your professionalism and ultimately give you a point of difference
- 🔒 Your video (if done properly) can be used as an example to other businesses
- 🔒 It is yet another opportunity to improve upon Search Engine Optimisation

<112>

21. Showcase sold properties

By showcasing your sold properties through video, you are inspiring sellers with confidence in your ability to sell and it provides you with yet another opportunity to create top of mind awareness for your business.

Benefits to you and your agency

- Dominate YouTube
- Improve Search Engine Optimisation
- Inspire sellers and create top of mind awareness
- It's your video resume

22. Gifts for sellers once house has been sold

Whilst some agents may provide gifts to sellers upon settlement, as always we should be seeking to create a lasting impression and a point of difference. What better way than providing them with a video of this significant point in their lives.

These videos, if done with care and special attention, are often accepted with great joy and appreciation.

Benefits to you and your agency

Benefits include:

- It is a memento to keep
- It can add value for your client
- It is a point of difference for your business
- It helps to create the 'wow' factor
- It's practically free

23. Weekly market updates

While frequency of contact is important, what is equally important is that this contact is relevant, useful and is done professionally. A weekly newsletter and market update will quickly turn into spam if you don't make sure that information is useful, current, informative and interesting.

Video is a little-used, yet extremely effective means of providing up-to-date and entertaining information.

Benefits to you and your agency

Benefits include:

- 🔒 It is an entertaining and useful form of communication
- 🔒 It is different to most other weekly updates or newsletters
- 🔒 It is a point of difference for your business
- 🔒 It helps to create the 'wow' factor
- 🔒 It can be topical
- 🔒 It is very inexpensive

24. How to use videos on job sites

Some job sites offer an opportunity to place videos that allow a business or employer to market themselves or describe the position in greater detail.

In order to attract the best, you have to present yourself as the best.

<114>

Benefits to you and your agency

Benefits include:

- 🔒 It is different to most other job ads so will attract more interest and high calibre applicants

- 🔒 It is a point of difference for your business and actually demonstrates your business positioning more than words alone

- 🔒 It helps to create a 'wow' factor

Secret Agents are their Brand.

<115>

Conclusion

What you have just read will dramatically assist you to build the profile you need to become known in your area.

This is everything you require to build massive online marketing momentum and ensure you have a wonderful career in real estate.

I wish each and every one of you all the best – and please keep in touch.

Lisa

If you would like to participate in our ten-week marketing course, please go to

Real Estate Marketing Academy

www.realestatemarketingacademy.com.au

If we all did the things we are capable of, we would literally astound ourselves.

—Thomas Edison

About the Author

Lisa B. is passionate about sourcing the latest and best information to train real estate agents to better use social media, video marketing, blogs and technology relating to real estate online marketing, with the sole purpose of getting more listings and making more sales.

Lisa started in real estate in the early 1990s and has owned and operated a number of successful real estate businesses. Initially part of a large franchise group, she then became an independent. This gave her the inspiration to study marketing in great detail, learning from the best in the world. Among other things, she learned how to promote her name and her company name.

Unlike some other real estate social media and digital marketing trainers, Lisa has implemented these strategies into her own business so she knows what works (and, equally importantly, what doesn't work). She now has critical information to share with you that will change your business life forever.

Lisa provides coaching, runs her own events (all have been sold out) and has spoken at many real estate conferences.

If you are looking for the edge on your competitors, and a real point of difference in your marketplace, Lisa can show you some clear and easy strategies to help you land on page one of the search engines.

<119>

A bit more information about Lisa

- 🔒 Creator of The Real Estate Hotline
- 🔒 Real Estate Online Marketing Specialist - Trainer and Speaker
- 🔒 Author of *Secret Agents*
- 🔒 Creator of Real Estate Marketing Academy Online Course
- 🔒 Licensed real estate agent since 1995
- 🔒 Since the early 1990s has owned and operated multiple real estate businesses
- 🔒 Won numerous awards for marketing and sales
- 🔒 Accredited life coach
- 🔒 NLP Master Practitioner
- 🔒 Justice of the Peace
- 🔒 Has had own column in numerous real estate magazines
- 🔒 Co-author of the bestselling book *Real Estate Millionaire*

If you want to learn more strategies using real estate social media, and how to position yourself and/or your company as the expert in your area in a simple, easy way, then go to
www.TheRealEstateHotline.com.au

<120>

Secret Agents don't worry about what went wrong yesterday;

they learn from it and then plan the next deliberate step.

<121>

To continue with your online training please join
our 10-week course.

For more details go to
www.realestatemarketingacademy.com.au

Keep in touch with Lisa B

LinkedIn –
www.linkedin.com/in/lisab007

Facebook –
www.facebook.com/groups/
LetsTalkAboutRealEstate

Twitter –
www.twitter.com/socialmediaRE1

Instagram –
www.instagram.com/lisab_author/

Pinterest –
au.pinterest.com/lisab007/

YouTube –
www.youtube.com/dominatetheinternet

<123>

Lack of direction, not lack of time, is the problem. We all have twenty-four hour days.

— Zig Ziglar

www.TheRealEstateHotline.com.au

NOTES

www.ingramcontent.com/pod-product-compliance
Lightning Source LLC
Chambersburg PA
CBHW071702210326
41597CB00017B/2292